CU00894742

THIS IS ME

I AM...

INNER VOICES

Edited By Lynsey Evans

First published in Great Britain in 2024 by:

Young Writers
Remus House
Coltsfoot Drive
Peterborough
PE2 9BF
Telephone: 01733 890066
Website: www.youngwriters.co.uk

Printed and bound in the UK by BookPrintingUK
Website: www.bookprintinguk.com
YB0576N

AMBITIOUS
OPTIMISTIC
LONELY
CREATIVE
KIND
PROUD
ANGRY
SHY HAPPY
LOYAL ANXIOUS
PASSIONATE
CONFIDENT
STRONG
ADVENTUROUS
BRAVE BORED
FEARLESS
SENSITIVE
EXTROVERTED
INTROVERTED
SAD STRESSED
AFRAID
MISUNDERSTOOD
FRUSTRATED

FOREWORD

Since 1991, here at Young Writers we have celebrated the awesome power of creative writing, especially in young adults where it can serve as a vital method of expressing their emotions and views about the world around them. In every poem we see the effort and thought that each student published in this book has put into their work and by creating this anthology we hope to encourage them further with the ultimate goal of sparking a life-long love of writing.

Our latest competition for secondary school students, This Is Me: I Am…, challenged young writers to write about themselves, considering what makes them unique and expressing themselves freely and honestly, something which is so important for these young adults to feel confident and listened to. There were no restrictions on style or subject so you will find an anthology brimming with a variety of poetic styles and topics. We hope you find it as absorbing as we have.

We encourage young writers to express themselves and address subjects that matter to them, which sometimes means writing about sensitive or contentious topics. If you have been affected by any issues raised in this book, details on where to find help can be found at www.youngwriters.co.uk/info/other/contact-lines

CONTENTS

Looe Community Academy, East Looe

Keeley Sleeman (13)	61
Freya Leanner (12)	62
Eliza Woollaston (13)	64
M. J. Lees (12)	65
Isaac Provost (12)	66
Lauren Williams (12)	67
Percy Casson (12)	68
Zane Moore (12)	69

Moorside High School, Swinton

Alina Kharsieua (14)	70
Ajab Fabeeh (12)	72
Iona Duncan (11)	73
Chloe Grounds (11)	74
Ollie Knowles-Clarke (11)	76
Nazly Musa (11)	77
Faa-iz Yahaya (11)	78
George Harrison (12)	79
Bella Gagan (11)	80
Emilia McDonald (11)	81

NET Red House Academy, Sunderland

Grace Wallace (11)	82
Logan Percy (11)	83
Josie Ditchburn (11)	84
Sarlote Millere (11)	85
Ahmed Alderi (12)	86
Zion Akinola (12)	87
Isaac Powell (11)	88
Deacon Stokell	89
Sofia Brown (11)	90
Dylan Davidson (12)	91
Ojuurereoluwa Akinola (12)	92
Lilia Devlin (11)	93
Lilly Mooney (11)	94
Aiden Leary (12)	95
Logan Morritt (13)	96
Jake Cockton (11)	97

Michael Jordan (13)	98
David Ladipo (12)	99
Isla Jackson (11)	100
Lucas Jarvis (11)	101
Rebecca Ellison (13)	102
Jack Eagling (11)	103
Owen Sheldon (13)	104
Lena Pawlowska (12)	105
Riley Naugher (11)	106
Lacey McCully (12)	107
Oliver Rose (12)	108
Kai (11)	109
Fletcher Murphy (11)	110
Jake Potts (11)	111
Jamie Hourigan (12)	112
Chloe Phuprate (13)	113
Shalom Oyebanji (12)	114
Romany Cruddas (11)	115
Jessica Fenwick (12)	116
Miley Middlemiss (12)	117
Vincent Gowland (12)	118
Usha Quinn (11)	119
Eden Lilli Sampson (13)	120
Johnjoe McKennell (13)	121

Ormiston Horizon Academy, Tunstall

Maisie Lowe (11)	122
Charlotte Henshall (12)	123
Troy Campbell (11)	124
Elizabeth May Walley (11)	126
Lucas Austin-Broomhall (12)	127
Chelsea Ferris (11)	128
Lola Mason (12)	130
Benjamin Burrows (12)	131
Isabella Allcock (12)	132
Liam Twardochleb (12)	133
Hannelore Makamure (11)	134
Deacon Grocott (12)	135
Marvelous Samuel (11)	136
Damien Oliveira (13)	137
Sophia Lowe (11)	138
Zedekiah Nasau	139

Outwood Academy Bydales, Marske-By-The-Sea

Preston School Academy, Yeovil

St Thomas Aquinas Secondary School, Glasgow

The Read School, Drax

Thetford Grammar School, Thetford

Wadham School, Crewkerne

Elsa Buckland (12)	213
Poppy Hale (11)	214
Hollie Difford (11)	216
Phoebe Curtis (11)	217
Charlie Hughes (11)	218
Sienna Madgin (11)	219
Ella Priddle (11)	220
Edie Pattisson	222
Poppy Dennis (11)	223
Darcie Charlton (12)	224
Arabella Linten (11)	225
Oliver Newbery (12)	226
Mykie Greenhill (14)	227
Katelin White (12)	228
Leah Coombes (12)	229
Isaac Galfin (13)	230
Sophie Venn (12)	231
Stanley Glover (13)	232
Faith Parsons (13)	233
Carl Bowles (15)	234
Caleb Russell (12)	235
Sami Malik (11)	236
Jack Smith (12)	237

DIFFERENT RELAXED
STRONG FIERCE
OPTIMISTIC
PASSIONATE
ANXIOUS

FUN LONELY
POSITIVE
ADVENTUROUS
HAPPY

THE
POEMS

EXTROVERTED
FEARLESS
LOYAL
MISUNDERSTOOD
GRATEFUL
STRONG
UPBEAT

OK
FINE
TOUGH
BORED
SAD
WISE
CHILL
BRAVE
KIND
WISE
QUIET

STRESSED
AMBITIOUS
ANGRY
PROUD
INTROVERTED
ENERGETIC
TRUSTWORTHY

Me

	P	urple, red, dark blue, they're my favourite colours
	E	ating is my favourite thing to do in my spare time
	A	SMR makes me calm like I'm on a cloud
	R	abbits and otters are my favourite animals
	L	ove swimming. I'm like an otter speeding in the water

	D	aisy and Abel are my sister and brother
b	O	rn in Lancaster... I'm the only one
p	U	mpkin carving and trick or treating are my favourite things to do at Halloween
	G	lasses - I wear them to help me see
	L	oveable. I love giving hugs to friends and family
H	A	rry Potter is what I love. Sometimes I feel like I'm in Hogwarts
	S	unny and always smiling.

Pearl Douglas (11)
Cartmel Priory CE School, Cartmel

Untitled

Now what can I tell you about me?
There's not much to tell but there's not much to say
about anyone,
Yes, I know there's the needy and the rich,
But no one really cares though,
They just say 'aw' and 'how lucky you are' to not be in
their shoes,
But they don't do anything!
No one really cares about this lousy little poem, do they?
Yes! They do; my poem isn't just what I feel,
I'm sharing my emotions with thousands of other people,
Who feel just the same as I do!
For me I love dogs,
I love to watch the sunset,
I enjoy swimming and jumping off cliffs!
Thousands of you will feel the same,
So don't think 'Oh, this is just some lousy poem'
When in my eyes it's me saying how I truly feel!
Most people write poems and express their emotions,
Which is what I'm doing,
But I'm guessing you don't think so,
Don't give up on a passion you may have!
Like I say, if you give up on something you're giving
up on the career,
But why do people give up?

Are they afraid to face what might come ahead in
the future?
No one truly knows, not even you,
This poem was meant to be about me, and it is,
It's just not like others, I guess you could say I'm unique,
Just like you!
When you have a passion, go for it,
Keep going no matter what anyone else says,
It's you against the world some days,
But that's okay, it shows who you truly are,
In the best way there can be!

Maddie Duggan (12)
Cartmel Priory CE School, Cartmel

I've Never Been Afraid To Be Me

When I was one,
I liked playing on my baby mat
When I was two,
I liked sitting in my pram and looking at horses in fields
When I was three,
I liked painting with my hands
When I was four,
I noticed a bump on my mum's tummy
When I was five,
A human smaller than me came along
When I was six,
All of the attention was on my little sister and I had
started a new year at school
When I was seven,
I was in year three,
My sister got older and she could stand up and walk
When I was eight,
I spoke my mind and gave my opinions, people wanted
to be my friend
When I was nine,
I learned about secondary, I got worried about my future
When I was ten,

I started liking football and I joined a team and started
playing for them
And now I'm eleven
And I'm not afraid to be my crazy, funny, friendly, loving self.

Lily Edmondson
Cartmel Priory CE School, Cartmel

Hi, I'm Me

Hi, I'm me,
There is no one else like thee.
I'm different
I'm unique
I'm exhilarant
A bit of cheek.

Hi, I'm me,
There is no one else like thee.
Some days I'm loud
Some days I'm quiet.
Some days I feel proud
Others I feel tired.

Hi, I'm me,
There is no one else like thee.
Despise clowns I do
Love meeting someone new
Climate change worries me
I think all animals should be free.

Hi, I'm me,
My name is Ruby.
Friends make me joyful
And family too
I like people who are loyal
And the people that are true.

I have to say,
I can make a stand,
I don't have to obey,
I don't have to command.

Hi, I'm me.
There will never be someone quite like
Me!

Ruby Boniface (13)
Cartmel Priory CE School, Cartmel

This Is Me

Optimistic, joyful, loyal and proud,
These are things that make me stand out in the crowd.
My life is sporty, I like skiing and swimming,
I'm quite competitive and so keen on winning!
I am quite relaxed, along with my mum and dad,
But my sister, on the other hand, she's really quite mad!
I also like Harry Potter, all the action and the fun,
There's nothing like it, honestly, there's none!
I am interested in music, and genres like rock and pop,
But I'm probably not the biggest fan of hip-hop!
My life is brilliant and yes, it can be busy,
And sometimes it does make me quite dizzy!
So that's my life as a whole for you,
I hope you like my poem too!

Max Crompton (11)
Cartmel Priory CE School, Cartmel

This Is Me

I strum my guitar, creating tunes,
In the morning and the evening nights.
I ride the snow, on my epic board,
Riding down hills, not bored.

I have a bike, I ride through the green,
Fast on trails, hard to be seen.
I like climbing the rocks, with all my might,
I never get a fright.

With tools, I build sick stuff,
Engineering things, fast and tough.
I wear a cap, it's my cool style,
Black and white like the sky in the night.

I love the outdoors, it's my big playground,
With so much to do, fun's always found.
I'm just a kid, with a wandering mind,
Living every day an adventurous life!

Ben Clarke (11)
Cartmel Priory CE School, Cartmel

This Is Me

I'm a human, I live in the world.
I am a human who believes you can do anything
If you put your mind to it.
I am a human who believes
If you give up, you come back even stronger.
I'm the person who
If you're struggling to do something
You ask for help
And don't let yourself be frightened
And let you become your true self
And help others
When they truly need the courage and endurance.
I'm the person who is a leader
And you can be one too
If you show strength, happiness
And you help others.
I'm the person who's there
If you need to have a laugh with someone.
I'm the person who will be kind and support you.

Zachary Rowlandson-Benson

Cartmel Priory CE School, Cartmel

What Makes Me

This is me.

I love my horses named
Freddie and Governor
Though they may bite and
Fight with one another.

I love music, it makes me
Feel safe when the
Problems I buried climb
Up from their grave.

I love to ride at Bigland.
Prince is my favourite!
Even if he bucks and
Rears; he licks my hands
To try and find treats.

And when I'm down and
Blue, the thing that I do is
Watch people online that
Play games, or hang out
With friends and just do
Stupid things.

This is what makes me, me.

Evie Jessett (13)
Cartmel Priory CE School, Cartmel

I Am Me!

I am me.
I like green,
I like blue,
I have a dog,
I like skiing too.
I am Jack.

I am me.
I do hobbies,
I do orienteering,
I do sport,
I do gaming
And I like music.

I am me.
I like food,
Pizza and chips,
Toad in the hole to pasta.
I like drinks,
Fanta and more.
Me is unique.

I am me.
I have my beliefs,
I have knowledge,
I have memories, good and bad,
Me is special.

I am me.
I am intelligent,
I am kind,
I am amazing.
Everything is great.

I am me.

Jack J (13)
Cartmel Priory CE School, Cartmel

I'm A Girl

I'm a girl but not girly
I like walking at sunset
I like horror movies
I like my quad bike
I'm a girl
I like law shows
I like farming a lot
I'm young and happy
I'm a girl
I like woods
I like home
I am me
I like Lana del Rey a lot
I'm creative
I am me
I like swimming
I like music
I like my family
I like nature
I like getting muddy
I am me
I like my friends
I like my bed
I like Harry Potter

I am me
I'm not girly
But I am a girl.

Meredith Whitton (12)
Cartmel Priory CE School, Cartmel

I Am Unique

I am unique,
And I'm not tall,
Sometimes I'm strong,
But sometimes I fall,
I am a dancer,
I follow my feet,
I have the whole world behind me,
I'm cute and sweet,
Sometimes I'm confident,
I reach for the stars,
I love animals,
And chocolate bars,
I love my friends,
And my family,
Sometimes I'm sad,
But mostly happy,
I'm not fast,
Or sporty,
If you watch me run,
You will agree,
I am funny,
24/7,
I'm mysterious and random,
And only 11...

Willow Parker (11)
Cartmel Priory CE School, Cartmel

Feelings

I am nothing
I have no true purpose
I am...
Worthless, I am
Outrageous, I am
Rude, I am
Tragic, I am
Heartless
Lazy, I am
Embarrassing, I am
Strange, I am
Sad
But now that I have gained friends,
and have begun to tell them how I feel,
I feel happier
I feel
Perfect, I feel
Exciting to see, I feel
Radiant, I feel
Fabulous, I feel
Extravagant, I feel
Courageous, I feel
Terrific
I am perfect, I am me.

Eleanor Ashworth (11)
Cartmel Priory CE School, Cartmel

This Is Me

I like sport,
Football is my thing,
It keeps me happy,
Takes my mind off things,
I play golf,
Swinging the club back and forth,
Hitting the ball far sometimes,
I like to skateboard,
Go out with friends,
Playing games,
I love going out at weekends,
I love spending time with my family,
They are so fun and happy,
I like going on calls with my friends after school,
Chatting and playing,
I love to play FIFA 24, it's so fun.

Mason Barrett (12)
Cartmel Priory CE School, Cartmel

My View Of The World

I'm a dancer,
I have tiny feet,
I think I'm strong,
But mainly weak.
My favourite month of the year is May
I came here because I have something to say...
The world is dying,
Because of us.
Animals are crying,
Below and above.
Do you ever think of turtles
Or birds up high?
Trees are being chopped down,
The cutters say goodbye.
That is my view of the world,
Says she.
I am who I want to be.

Alice Baddeley (11)
Cartmel Priory CE School, Cartmel

This Is Me

Bubbly and beautiful,
My colour is lavender,
My pets are cats, dogs and snakes too,
My animal is a lynx.
Bubbly and beautiful,
Bubbly and beautiful I am,
My sister is called Sky,
My passion is drama,
My friendships have a strong bond.
Bubbly and beautiful,
Bubbly and beautiful I am,
My home town is Grange,
My country is England,
My life is perfect.
Bubbly and beautiful,
Bubbly and beautiful I am.

Mia Atkinson (11)

Cartmel Priory CE School, Cartmel

This Is Me

I like football
Being in a team with my friends.
I like fishing,
The calm, peaceful nature.
I like biking,
It's scary but fun.
I like my friends,
Meeting and having fun.
I like my family,
How nice they are to me.
I like to play on my Xbox,
It is fun with my friends.
I like autumn,
All the crispy leaves.
I like DT,
Making cool things.
I like the Earth,
All the nice places.

Alfie Richards (13)
Cartmel Priory CE School, Cartmel

This Is Me

I love to go shooting, the smell of the fresh shot cartridge
I love to do fishing, the swaying of water
I love to play instruments and the beautiful
harmonious sound
I love to spend time with my family, they are so much fun.
I love to play Red Dead Redemption 2 with Alfie Richards
I love to play Seige too, it makes me cry
I love to play Hunter Call of the Wild. It is really fun
I love life.

Mikey Anderson (12)
Cartmel Priory CE School, Cartmel

Poem For Me

E nergetic, I am as energetic as a cheetah.
L oyal, I am as loyal as a lion.
O bservant, I am as observant as a gecko.
I ntelligent, I am as intelligent as a parrot.
S pectacular, I am as spectacular as a spider.
E xcellent, I am as excellent as a swan.

Eloise Gemmell (12)
Cartmel Priory CE School, Cartmel

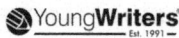

I Am Robert

I am **R** obert
I am **O** blivious
I am **B** rilliant
I am **E** nergetic
I am **R** eal
I am **T** ired

I am **W** arren
I am **A** dventurous
I am **R** eady
I am **R** estless
I am **E** xcellent
I am **N** atural.

Robert Warren (13)
Cartmel Priory CE School, Cartmel

Nobody Can Stop Me

You are unique
Your courage is like a mountain peak
So high, nobody can reach
Spend all day on a warm, sunny beach
Everyone has a superpower
I bloom like a sweet-scented flower
Higher than a tree, higher than a
mountain until Mars I will see
Nobody can stop me.

Alicja Krepa
Cartmel Priory CE School, Cartmel

Who I Am

I am amazing
I can do this
I can push through
I am adventurous
I am good at this
I am passionate
I am me!
I am funny
I make people laugh
I like music
Music likes me
These are the things that make me, me!

Archie Sykes (11)

Cartmel Priory CE School, Cartmel

It's Me

It's me
I like pink and teal
It's me
It's me
I like cats and dogs
I like creativity, adventures
It's me
I like when people are funny and kind
It's me
And this is me.

Lily Haslam (11)
Cartmel Priory CE School, Cartmel

This Is Me

I may be small,
Of all the people tall,
But one little thing can make a difference,
No matter the age or height,
Race or might,
I will be myself,
Because I should show the world,
This is me.

Robbie Brown (12)
Cartmel Priory CE School, Cartmel

This Is Me

I'm shy and happy and fun
I'm frail and fast and dumb
I am very crafty and very neat
I am rhythmic and very kind
I am very sweet
And I really like to eat
M&M's are good
I scoff them down
Very good.

Maddison Wadlow (11)
Cartmel Priory CE School, Cartmel

This Is Me

This is me...
I am... tired
I am... a gamer
I am... a boxer
I fight for strength
I am... a fighter
I am... forgetful
I forget to sleep
I am... tired
I am... idiotic
I am... funny
I love to laugh.

Reuben Marsh (13)
Cartmel Priory CE School, Cartmel

My Refuge

You tell me you love me
Wish me immortality
You whisper, "Be selfish,
Allow yourself this time to cherish."

But Daddy, we've eons to share
Why rant of such despair?
O Daddy, that seraphic smile
Do wear it while we walk the aisle.

Allow me our dream-like dance
I'll provide you your second chance
Grant me thy sacred speech
While we stand, together on that beach.

Daddy? Did you hear that bell-like sound?
Is that why you let Him slip off your crown?
Tell me, you only just left town,
Please, don't leave me alone in this gown.

Amy Whitefield (16)
Durham School, Durham

Sycamore Gap

I'm just a tree,
Sycamore Gap, I'm called,
Nothing special, not worthy,
When summer fades, I'm completely bald,
Yet, am I loved?

By the people, the wind whistles,
The selfish terrifying tribe,
I am like a thistle,
Dull, no eye-catching vibe,
What do they see?

Fiancés propose right in front of my eyes,
Elders leave gifts by my feet,
Many lie under my roof and gaze up at the night skies,
To escape reality, to feel complete,
Yet still I am just a tree,
Am I loved?

Then one night, two people came,
Storm Agnes,
She blew a great storm my way but I won the game,
But something else came that night,
A cosmic beast. Could you guess?

A human, what a sight,
He arrived, I thought maybe for some peace,
He had no peace in those 'eyes',
Hate was inscribed onto his paper face,
And then it happened,
Is it the end?

It was so quick,
I wasn't ready to go,
He pierced this venomous weapon straight through my
hollow heart,
A single sycamore fell from my branch,
Now I must part,
Will I be missed?

As I fall to the soft pillow,
I take my last breath,
Was I a hero?

The Sycamore Gap no more,
The gap in our hearts,
Just a tree?
You were so much more,
Did you know that?

Matilda Costello (13)
Durham School, Durham

Sirens

Sirens - all hope lost
Sirens - the dreaded sound
Sirens - all hope lost
Sirens - pray to be found

Safety - there's no chance
Safety - that's the past
Safety - there's no chance
Safety - over fast

Hiding - help me now
Hiding - can't get out
Hiding - help me now
Hiding - hear me shout

Stranded - on my own
Stranded - I am gone
Stranded - on my own
Stranded - life goes on

Sirens - all hope lost
Sirens - the dreaded sound
Sirens - all hope lost
Sirens - I am found.

Rosie McDonald (15) & Amy Gatland (14)
Durham School, Durham

Refuge

Everyone seeks a bit of refuge,
They sometimes end up in a centrifuge.

Everyone seeks a safe haven,
All people from different associations.

Some travel to another nation,
Which can be a big operation.

Some people enjoy the pain,
Although, most are never the same.

Your home is a place away from threat,
A place you should not regret.

Everyone seeks to have a shelter,
And it is always for the better.

Refuge is a serious thing,
That does not only belong to a king.

Gustav Bergenstjerna (14)
Durham School, Durham

All Is Forgotten

Lungs desperate for air.
Ears desperate for silence.
Mind desperate for calm.
Heart desperate for comfort.

Running for peace.
Running for refuge.

Until finally...
Air.
Silence.
Calm.
Comfort.

In the garden, all is forgotten.

The scent of lavender enfolds me.
Birdsong soothes my troubled mind.
The old oak leans in to offer solace.
Vibrant flowers brighten the gloom.

Nature is my haven.

James Turner (14)
Durham School, Durham

Refuge

Escape the danger and the attack
Leave home and don't turn back
Seek refuge far and wide
A safe haven from outside.

No more need for fear
Don't you shed a tear
Seek refuge far and wide
A safe haven from outside.

Darcy Holmes (14)
Durham School, Durham

Refuge In Books

Opening the cover
Reading the page
Feeling the paper
Loving the book.

Opening the cover
Reading the heart
Feeling the harmony
Loving the book.

Becoming myself.

Freya Mole (14)
Durham School, Durham

The Me Inside Of Me

I solemnly walk down the hall
Running my nails across the tiled wall
Every person unaware
That the me they see isn't really there
I turn the key, open the door
Toss my bag down on the floor
Why can't anyone simply see
The me inside of me?

I've left the horrible dingy school
Left all the faces they deemed cool
The me they see isn't really me
The real me is drowning in the sea
A sea of fears and expectations
Drowning in my trepidations
Fears that if they really knew
They wouldn't like the you inside of you.

They'd think you weird, poke you with pins
Commend you for their own dastardly sins
Experiment on your strange green arms
Thinking you intend them harm
For I'm piloting a big machine
Sat in the head, empty and clean
An alien finally they'd see
That's the me inside of me.

Charlotte Grierson (15)
Garstang Community Academy, Garstang

Me!

What do I like in my life?
I like the sports like the swish of a hockey stick
or the dribble of a basketball
It doesn't matter if I'm short or tall!
The whack of the ball in the back of the net
I will play in dry and wet
The tap of a shoe, the dance begins
Swishing and swaying to the sound of the song
Splash of water as I swim
Going from start to end like a mermaid in the sea
I love my family and my friends
They mean the world to me
This is me!

Eve Robinson (12)

Garstang Community Academy, Garstang

Flowing With You

My life flows steadily like water,
My life thrashes and crashes like waves,
Sometimes it drips slowly and painfully,
And sometimes, it crushes me like a waterfall.
Sometimes I lose myself under stress like a current,
And sometimes it streams down my cheeks,
And other times I worry I will evaporate and won't
be here for you anymore.
But most of the time I'm calm, flowing steady with you.

Tilly Rafferty (13)
Garstang Community Academy, Garstang

Free My Mind

Maybe I should write about my imagination,
Something about my nation,
I need to let my mind free,
Writing about a busy, buzzing bee.
All of these rules,
Are keeping me locked,
Outside of the creative world,
I'm stuck next to a tick-tocking clock,
All I'm trying to do is free my mind,
But all of the noise is happening from behind!

Beth Slater (13)
Garstang Community Academy, Garstang

Free My Mind

Maybe I should write about my imagination
Or something about my nation?
I need to set my mind free,
Writing about silly, crazy me.
All of these rules,
Are keeping me locked up,
I have no idea what to do,
Because all my thoughts are quite new.
I think I'm ready to free my mind,
And show all people how to shine!

Erica Purnell (12)
Garstang Community Academy, Garstang

The Power Of Sport

Cycling is the best sport in the world
Just let your greatness unfurl
Racing at top speed
Putting your team in the lead
All your thoughts are forgotten
As you fly down a hill to the bottom
Speeding at forty miles an hour
Only then will you hold the power.

Abby Johnston (15)
Garstang Community Academy, Garstang

The Silver Trophy

I am a trophy, I'm made out of silver
I make people winners, I make people's wishes come true
I bring joy in lives but... It only lasts a while
They keep me, look at me for a day or two
Then... forget me. They don't look at me or touch me
I feel so desolate, I made you happy and
You made me sad and feel tormented...
But it's okay...
I've already gotten my revenge
The day you got me, many were jealous, many were sad
Many decided to hate you and some became backstabbers
Now, they won't be the same as they used to be
Thanks to me, you're now at war.

Do let me know how it feels to be alone.

Samrit Kaur (13)
Joseph Leckie Academy, Walsall

Bottles Of Paint

I am a bottle of paint
There are multiple of me
I have the use of creativity

Roses are red
Violets are blue
I have multiple uses
But you can choose one to do

I am a bottle of paint
There are many things you can do with me,
Paint a face, paint a picture, paint a landscape

I am a bottle of paint
There are many different shades of me
But they aren't as strong to cure a terminal disease.
Children who use me,
I make them happy,
But they would want to use me over and over again

I am a bottle of paint
I help children create things like sunsets,
Rainbows and happy endings.

Phoebe Cooper (13)
Joseph Leckie Academy, Walsall

I Am A Pencil

I am a pencil
Made of lead as grey as the cloudy skies
And wood that is harder than a rock.
When they sharpen me, my skin gets cut off.
My biggest enemy is the sharpener.
I can write numbers
I can write words
I can write sentences
I write people's feelings, fears and thoughts, yet I can't write mine.
I draw things and people, but the rubber always rubs out my work,
So I have to start again.
People lose me all the time.
People shrink me until they don't need me and have nothing left.
I sometimes feel worthless and that one day I'll disappear.

Noor Zaman (13)
Joseph Leckie Academy, Walsall

Cover Me Up

I am there to make young girls feel beautiful
And help clowns paint smiles on their faces
However, sometimes I can't cover their pain or wrinkles
I cover up people's insecurities with confidence
But no one will ever know how they feel on the inside
Like a celebrity using a filter
No matter how much make-up people use
It will never truly cover up their real pain
I can make people feel like a model
Just by using a bottle
From different brushes to sponges
I can cover most of your insecurities.

Humna Nasar (13)
Joseph Leckie Academy, Walsall

Shattered Glass

I am hard on the outside
And soft on the inside
I am like a piece of glass
I am handling so much on the outside
But slowly, I am breaking down on the inside
Just like a glass cup
If you break me, I'll shatter into a million pieces
That could never be the same again
Just like a piece of glass
Most of the time, I feel like everyone can see through me
Just like I'm transparent
If you break me, I'll break down with others
I try to prevent it but that is just who I am.

Fabiha Sultana (13)
Joseph Leckie Academy, Walsall

Shadows

I'm a shadow,
I see it all,
I'm a bad copy of everything.
I need light to be seen,
When I can be seen, no one cares.
They walk past and all over me,
As if I'm nothing,
Like I'm not even there,
Even though they look at me,
They leave me.
But, when in the dark,
They fear me.
As I sit in the corner,
Like I'm something to fear,
The children sometimes play with me,
Some run from me.
But, in the end, they forget me,
As I'm a shadow.

Elsie Cronin (14)
Joseph Leckie Academy, Walsall

Kettle

I am a kettle,
Sweet as a petal,
Made of a button and a pot.
I get annoyed when people push my buttons,
And that makes my blood start to pop.
When I get angry,
My steam and bubbling blood could burn you.
When my pot is empty, I feel lonely,
But when it's full, that's not good.
I'm serious, smart and stubborn
But still, millions and millions of people around the world
Use me.
This is how I am a kettle
And sweet as a petal.

Saira Hamidi (13)
Joseph Leckie Academy, Walsall

Friendly Magnet

I am a magnet,
Made out of metal,
With no heart,
But if you put two ends of me, the opposite I attract.

But sorry, I am not as friendly to stick with my twin,
As I am always fighting with him.

I can be pretty or simple,
Stay still like a tiny statue or a symbol,
A million times people forget I am there,
And even when they look at me,
They do without care!
But this doesn't matter;
I know I am better.

Eliana Murati (13)
Joseph Leckie Academy, Walsall

I Am A Star

I am a star.
I am a star.
I am bright.
I am bright like a light.
I shine.
I shine in the sky in the night.
I have five sharp corners like a knife.
I am untouchable.
I am unbreakable like a rock.
I am a star.
I am a star.
I am bright like a light.
I am beautiful like a flower.
I have a power.
I have the power of shining.
I am a star.
I am a star.
I am bright like a light.

Areebah Hassan (13)
Joseph Leckie Academy, Walsall

Lonely Pot

I am a pot
I am used to cook food
You can't touch me when I'm hot
Because I will burn you
The fire hates me
Which is why it's so severe
I'm used for your food
And yet no one cares for me
I can cook
I can be washed
And yet I'm still punished by fire
After I'm used, I'm thrown in the cupboard
Waiting to be used again
I'm a pot
A lonely pot.

Roshda Irshad (13)
Joseph Leckie Academy, Walsall

I'm A Supercar

I am a supercar,
I can be fast or slow,
I am always a manual,
Tired or energetic,
I am a show-off when I want to be.
I am flashy,
And sometimes I'm clean or dirty,
I never break down.
I am used by the rich but not the poor,
Because the rich are getting rich and
The poor are getting poorer.
The point is, I'm not perfect.

Marquez Clarke (13)
Joseph Leckie Academy, Walsall

Bracelet

I am a bracelet
Made of diamonds
I have no feelings
Take me anywhere
I make you look good
Blingy, beautiful and bright, that's what I am
I am very stylish
I cost a lot
Do you think you can afford me?
I am used to make people happy
I am some people's dream
Some people would do anything to get me
I am a bracelet.

Avi Bal (14)

Joseph Leckie Academy, Walsall

I Am A Lock

I am a lock,
Hard as a rock,
Nothing can set me free,
Not even a key,
I grow in the most dark and depressing places,
Not even a bat can see,
So here as I sit with cat number three,
Life would be so much easier,
If there were two of me.

Ifrah Shazad (13)
Joseph Leckie Academy, Walsall

Glitter

I shine like stars in the midnight sky.
When I walk into a room, all the attention goes to me.
I make kids happy.
There is a bright smile when they see me.
I bring a lot of joy and happiness to kids' faces.

Sumaya Hossain (13)
Joseph Leckie Academy, Walsall

Flower

I am a flower,
I can be made into a bouquet,
I can make someone happy,
I can brighten your day,
People smile when they see me,
People give me as a sign of love,
People plant me but take my life away.

Raahina Karim (13)
Joseph Leckie Academy, Walsall

Money

I'm filthy like money,
I'm really funny when I get bored.
I spent some money.
I know I'm spoiled but I'm royal.
But sometimes I can be loyal.

Frankie Fellows (13)
Joseph Leckie Academy, Walsall

This Is Me

I sometimes get shy
I also love my friends
I sometimes take care of my brothers
And I love cookies.

I love chocolate
I also like writing
Sometimes, I get crazy
Sometimes, I get scared
And most of all, I like helping people.

Sometimes, I get shy
Sometimes, I get angry
I also like being proud
I also like being kind
I love English
And I love writing stories.

I love spending time with my pets
I love music
I love making people laugh
And I love art.

I like being funny
I like being loved
I like my friends
And I love being positive.

Keeley Sleeman (13)
Looe Community Academy, East Looe

I Am Me

I am me,
Kind,
Smart,
Funny,
I am me,
I may not be,
The kindest,
The smartest,
Or even the funniest,
But,
I am me,
I like who I am,
I'm thankful for who I am,
I do have a bad side but I don't like to show it,
I am me,
I do get scared,
I do get angry and quite often actually,
I do get shy but I don't like to show it,
I am me,
I don't find things in life easy but that's the way I like to live,
I do have a lot of family issues,
But,
I am me,
Every day I forget about it and still put a smile on my face,
And,

My life may not be perfect but that's what makes my life perfect,
For me,
Everything about me I like, no matter what,
I am still me.

Freya Leanner (12)
Looe Community Academy, East Looe

This Is Me

I wake up and crawl out of bed,
It feels like loads are in my head.
My heart feels heavy like a stack of bricks,
Is it me or a strange mix?
Then I walk over to a light switch,
Tap, tap, tap, and then I start to twitch.
ADHD,
Can't get the best of me.
When I'm with family,
I feel less tappy.
I get to the beach and get my board,
It makes me feel like I'm not so bored.
I feel more happy,
And much less tappy.
I try and try,
And I cry and cry.
But worries and anxiety,
Can't take my life from me!
Everyone is allowed to be different.

Eliza Woollaston (13)
Looe Community Academy, East Looe

This Is Me

I am as I am
Nobody can stop that
I am me because
Of all the things that make me
Well, me.

The top three things that make me are:
Godzilla, a fictional film character that I love,
From his atomic breath to his big body.
My friend Lauren is a great friend,
I can say the greatest friend I ever had.
And finally, the final thing that makes me is my dad,
He is the world's best dad,
He is like my hero,
Like Iron Man
Like Thor
Even like a Viking
He will be the best thing that makes me.

M. J. Lees (12)
Looe Community Academy, East Looe

These Bricks Are What Build Me

These bricks are what build me
And these bricks make me tall and stand me high
So high it makes skyscrapers look small.

These bricks express my feelings and personality
And these bricks keep getting better and stronger
And these bricks keep getting added on.

These bricks that I stand on are what I like the most
I like to dive on my jet ski and go surfing
I also like to play football, which is my favourite.

These are my bricks.

Isaac Provost (12)
Looe Community Academy, East Looe

Who Am I?

I am made of metal,
I like music, science, English, reading and maths
I am made of meatballs, chocolate, cake and food
Every day I smile and laugh,
I love science, music, English, Dachshunds and Labradors.
I like drawing, colouring and TV.
I love my brother,
I feel embarrassed and proud about my heart surgery.
It has made me feel energised.

Lauren Williams (12)
Looe Community Academy, East Looe

The Sea

There is no place I would rather be
Than out by the sea,
Hearing the waves splash cures anyone's gnarly gash!
Big waves make us dream big.
When I'm out on my surfboard,
Out at sea,
Everyone's problems disappear
When you're out at sea,
Topped off with a cheeky Nando's with the boys.

Percy Casson (12)
Looe Community Academy, East Looe

Who Am I?

I am short
Sometimes I am funny
I like taking life slowly.

My walls are my family
I love sushi
I am a short person.

Every day I say hello to my dogs
Often, I game
I am a short person.

Zane Moore (12)
Looe Community Academy, East Looe

The Girl That Made Many Mistakes

This is me,
The girl that made many mistakes,
In life, mistakes are woven, lessons unspoken.
Threads of imperfection and fault,
For humans are flawed beings,
I stumble and fall.
Yet mistakes don't define me, they're not my all.
I am human.

In the realm of errors, I often reside,
Since there, lies a second chance to shine.
Away from society's judgement, their harsh gaze,
Shame upon you, for every little slip.
Their disapproval, like a weight that grips,
I rise upon, with resilience and passion.
With empathy, I stay humble,
Knowing my mistakes don't define my worth.

In the realm of truth, I often reside,
Where mishaps are acknowledged,
Not denied.
For my errors are mere stepping stones,
Where growth intercepts.

Mistakes don't define me,
They're but a part,
Of my tapestry, my human art.
This is me.

Alina Kharsieua (14)
Moorside High School, Swinton

Rogue Planets

When I was a kid, I used to count backwards from ten,
And imagine when I got to one, there would be an explosion.
Perhaps caused by a rogue planet crashing into Earth,
Or some other major catastrophe.
When nothing happened, I'd be relieved,
And at the same time, a little disappointed.

I think of you at ten, the first time I saw you,
You smiled at nine, and how it lit up something inside me I
had thought long dead.
Your lips at eight pressed against mine,
And seven, your warm breath in my ear and your hands
everywhere.
You tell me you love me at six,
And at five, we have our first fight.
At four, we have our second,
And three, our third.
At two, you tell me you can't go on like this any longer,
And then at one, you ask me to stay.
And I am relieved, so relieved,
And a little disappointed.

Ajab Fabeeh (12)
Moorside High School, Swinton

72

Therian

You may dislike me, call me weird or fatherless,
But I will never stop being me.
I am a Therian,
It's my identity and belief.
I get barked at and meowed at,
But it will never hurt me.
I respect everyone I meet,
Can't you do this back?
I may have a mask and a tail,
But this is for comfort.
I promise to try hard at school,
Put 100% into all I do.
I am the same as everyone else,
Just get treated differently.
Wouldn't you feel like this too?
This is my message to the world,
Be yourself and don't make others feel bad for being them.
You can change the world,
Please try to understand Therians should be treated fairly.
I don't want to win, I want to educate!

Iona Duncan (11)
Moorside High School, Swinton

This Is Who I Am

Who am I?
I am a girl
I have brown hair and grey eyes
I am over five feet
I have glasses
This is who I am.

Who am I?
I am a lion, brave and strong
I am like a tiger, fierce and strong
I am creative and fun as well
This is who I am.

Who am I?
I am an actor
I am a chef
I am a songwriter
I am a charity worker
And I am an influencer
This is who I am.

Who am I?
I am a sister
I am a daughter
I am part of a family
This is who I am.

Who am I?
I'm not a liar
I'm not stupid
I am smart and truthful
This is who I am.

We are all different
And we are all amazing.

Chloe Grounds (11)
Moorside High School, Swinton

Ref! Are You Taking The Mick?

Our coach sent the message,
It's kick-off at 3.
It's a very big day,
For my team and me.
We're against top of the league today,
The whistle goes...
Let's play.
The ball is passed from left to right,
Up in the air,
Almost out of sight.
A foul has been given, and a free kick,
"*Ref!* Are you taking the mick?"
As I stand in my net, my heart beating fast,
I pray my defenders don't let that ball past.
He's gone for it, he's tried to score,
But I've saved it,
I want this more,
I pass to my striker,
There's another net to fill,
He shoots from 12 yards,
OMG... 1-nil.

Ollie Knowles-Clarke (11)
Moorside High School, Swinton

Self-Respect And Esteem

Let your heart's light shine through
And your confidence will thrive in you
I once was shy
But I let it pass by
I was walked all over on
And I was treated like a toy for fun
I let the world devour me
Swallowing me up, getting more and more filled with glee
I said a verse in my head
Multiple times it must be said
A heart can be broken
But can't be left unspoken
My trail was mazed
And my path was blazed
I didn't know what to do
The darkness was eating me through
I started to gain friends
And this has a happy end
You don't have to try so hard
To have a friend
'Cause truly good times never end.

Nazly Musa (11)
Moorside High School, Swinton

Attributes Of Victory

My name is Faa-iz,
Faa-iz means Victory,
I like reading and writing, maths and history,
To be a writer, I aspire,
To achieve this dream, I will not tire
At every opportunity, I'll make sure I'm up for hire,
I'm in a family of four,
We love each other so much more,
We are together forever through every door,
In every lesson, I study,
For every school day, I hurry,
For my lessons I'm nice and the teachers think I'm funny,
The attributes of me,
The attributes of Victory,
The attributes of who I am and who I want to be.

Faa-iz Yahaya (11)
Moorside High School, Swinton

Me! I Am Me!

Oh, life is life! But my life is wild!
You see, for six years I've been beaten to the crown
By fists and hurtful words, but one day I'll show them.
Yeah, I will show them what I'm made of!

I want to show the world what I can do!
To change the planet of entertainment, because I am me!
Because this is me!

See, my aunty has a deadly disease
And I want to do the best that I can to help her.
So for her sake, I'll show the world what I can do
And I'll do my best to succeed because
This is me, and I am me!

George Harrison (12)
Moorside High School, Swinton

All About Me

This is me and my life,
Art is one of my favourite subjects,
I also like writing whatever comes to mind,
I'm creative, I get inspired quickly!

I love reading and I get lost in my own world sometimes,
When I'm bored, I sometimes write stories or just draw,
I like dogs but my favourite breed is a Rottweiler,
I write things down fast or I might lose it.

I like hanging out in the school library because it helps me
relax and concentrate.

This is all about me.

Bella Gagan (11)
Moorside High School, Swinton

The Little Robin

A robin, a robin, I am a robin
Who sits on a branch of a tree
Listening to the sounds of the other birds
And lost in my imagination
A robin who sings along to the school bells
A robin as tiny as a robin can be, a robin.

I am a robin who doesn't want to win
But wants to write a nice poem for my nana's anniversary.

Emilia McDonald (11)
Moorside High School, Swinton

Untitled

The bricks that built me are,
My mum, dad, sister, brother, granda and nana,
I love being funny and fun,
I am made of being silly, fun and very, very daft,
"But are you?"
I hear you ask...
I'll tell you at the end.

I am topped off with school,
My walls are that I have a bad heart and have
a pacemaker in to make it beat better,
I take shelter under my mum because when I
need help or someone to go to,
I can go to her whenever I need someone.

At my core, you will find,
That I am helpful, kind, confident, annoying,
Loving, nice, mixed feelings, nosy
And I love my friends and family to bits,
You will also find a spark that will be shared.

I am Grace Wallace.

Grace Wallace (11)
NET Red House Academy, Sunderland

The Day I Woke Up

Although I am shy,
I like to see what's going on.
At my core, you will find a strong wild person.
As I seem strong, I am weak on the outside.
The will of my structure is hard to break.
As I am no sentry person,
I take shelter underneath the people who built me,
My mum and dad.
My dad taught me how to fish,
And though he had a lot of confidence he was overbold.
My mum taught me how to be wild and silly.
I'm normally shy and stay away from people
But when I'm ready I'll jump out and kill my prey.
Although my brother is annoying I will protect him,
Even though I'm weak on the inside.
When the dawn goes down in every morning,
In the night that's when you learn who I am.

Logan Percy (11)
NET Red House Academy, Sunderland

My 'All About Me' Poem

These are the bricks that built me.
I am really weird and really silly.
Sometimes I can be really daft.
Nearly every day, I get spoilt by my mam and dad.
I have mixed emotions when I'm in big crowds.
My mam taught me to cook to be independent
when I'm older.
My favourite food is mangos,
I'm not really a big fan of tomatoes.
I'm a freestyle dancer,
But when I was younger, I was always dancing and
I would sing all morning and night.
My mam loves it when I sing to her.
Once, my sister fell asleep watching me.
The most important thing about me is my dancing
and singing.
From today, I still dance and sing to my mam,
It's just who I am.

Josie Ditchburn (11)
NET Red House Academy, Sunderland

The Bricks That Built Me

I am made of these bricks:
Creative, loving, caring, funny at school
Because I like my friends
Kind, happy, confident all the time
Because I am always ready to answer a question
I like to draw every day because it makes me happy
I listen to music mostly when I am doing something
at home.

My hobbies are to sew, create something
Every day I go to a craft club
I learn lots of new skills for sewing
My two favourites are science and English
I take shelter under my mum when I feel sad, unhappy
Or when I need to talk to her about something upsetting
I am also lazy, sometimes sporty
I like to dance, I also like to play video games.

Sarlote Millere (11)
NET Red House Academy, Sunderland

Everyday Life

I wake up to the deafening sound of Bixby.
Telling me how hot or cold it is.
Or what the time is.
Or if it's going to rain or snow.
And then I have to push my lifeless body,
half-dead, out of my bed.
Trying not to miss the bus.
And when I go to school, it will be very cruel.

I go to period one, hoping this day would end.
Period two isn't any better.
My body is already beaten and battered by learning.
Midday, period three, is when I am completely numb.
When it ends and goes to period four, my soul gets
crushed by hunger.
Forced against my own will to wait.
Period five is the best when I know the day will end soon.

Ahmed Alderi (12)
NET Red House Academy, Sunderland

My Mystery

Every day, I wake up to a weak morning.
Thinking of how to make a smile on my face.
Which creates the spring up of the wired me.
My friends see me as a bad example of friendship.
I push forward, trying to forget about my past.
But in everything, my past still makes me.
My bricks get weaker and weaker.
Which I try to build.
Should I build myself back up?
Which makes me not care about what people say about me.
Then my pierced heart began to glue together.
And a strong person grows in me.
And accidentally, I came to understand.
And I began to see the other face of life.
This poem is about a boy called Ayobami Johnson.

Zion Akinola (12)
NET Red House Academy, Sunderland

This Is Me

These are the bricks that built me...
My mum who taught me how to cook,
Sister who taught me how to swim,
Dad who gives me pocket money,
Sunny as my nan.
Michael who taught me how to catch lobsters and crabs
And how to hold them.
Grandad who taught me how to fish
And how to put the bait, weights, hooks, loops, and the line.
I caught my first fish down at Roker Pier
Which was a mural.
My brother caught two
But I only caught one,
And it was the biggest and the longest.
I was so happy on the day.
I was so happy that I phoned my grandad and he
said, "Good."
And he gave me some pocket money.

Isaac Powell (11)
NET Red House Academy, Sunderland

Deacon's Boxing

I sat waiting to go to boxing for the first time
I sat lacing up my trainers
Ready for the first time until
I saw the car outside
My legs were trembling with fear
I crawled to the car and the next thing I knew
I was there
I slowly went up the stairs to see trophies on the wall
I looked inside and felt down
Until someone approached me
I recognised him
It was my friend, Brendon
I trained harder than ever
Until I walked back down the stairs again
But not alone
Until I left the gym for the first time
The wind hit my face for the first
But not the only time.

Deacon Stokell
NET Red House Academy, Sunderland

YoungWriters® Est. 1991

My Dance Life

At my core, you will find dance
I was three when I started
I don't know how I became obsessed
My dance team is basically my life beam
I was welcomed like I'd been there for ages
I was good friends with these two girls, Chloe and Olivia
Chloe left unfortunately
Covid came and me and Olivia didn't see each other
Until after Covid, which was a while
After Covid, we got put in groups
And I was in Bubble 2
My connection to dance was strong
Now I'm in Bubble 3, one of the older groups
I've been dancing for eight years now
And my connection stays strong.

Sofia Brown (11)
NET Red House Academy, Sunderland

Matchday Madness

Folks talking,
Folks predicting the scoreline for the match.
Heat was blazing in the halfway house.
Fellas laughing and playing pool.
Fans watching the other team's match.

30 minutes prior to kick-off,
5000 fans down Wessington Way.
The ten-minute walk to the Stadium of Light
means a lot to me.
3-0 the score should be.
"Get in. Come on lads. Ha'way the lads."

Jumping, shouting, and singing engulfed
the streets of Sunderland.
Music and cheering invaded Hastings Hill.
A walk home with a smile on my face.
That's the spirit!

Dylan Davidson (12)
NET Red House Academy, Sunderland

Poem About Me

Hi everyone.
I am here to say about me.
I grew up with a happy family.
This family gave me strong bricks,
Most of the time I do things and people think
I do it for no reason;
But later, the truth is revealed.
I have a calm spirit,
An always happy spirit,
I rarely get angry,
Which always keeps me
And makes me strong.
It helps me to overcome strong challenges in life,
With the love and support of my family.
I became an indestructible person in things,
Even when life wanted to keep me down.
My bricks stood as my shield.
That is all about me.

Ojuurereoluwa Akinola (12)
NET Red House Academy, Sunderland

This Is Me

These are the bricks that built me.
But one is the most important.
Ollie is a horse at EBRC.
He is one of the tallest horses,
And one of the skinniest as well.
I met him last month on a Thursday evening.
I was a little bit scared to ride him,
But once I got on and started cantering,
I didn't want to stop.
He has such a flowy trot,
Which is as smooth as a breeze.
He has made me feel so confident,
Which is so important to me.
I hope to ride him again.
Maybe next week?
But I hope I can loan him one day,
And feed him lots of treats.

Lilia Devlin (11)
NET Red House Academy, Sunderland

Lilly Story For The Start Of East Boldon Riding Centre

Inside my head, hay nets jump around
Before I leave to go home
Home, home away from home
Bridle, saddle, horse/pony
East Boldon, riding my home
From the start of day one
Learning to trot
To learning to canter
By my side every day, Bobby
To having my first fall
To having lots of falls
Meeting all the horses/ponies
Staff and friends
East Boldon, my best friend
For helping me get so far
I wouldn't get this far without the
horse/pony and staff
From now on, cantering/jumping games/shows
and lots more
Bobby.

Lilly Mooney (11)
NET Red House Academy, Sunderland

This Is Me

Hello, my name is Aiden, and I was born in 2011 on
the 1st of September.
I am really clumsy and I love football.
At the age of 1, I spoke my first ever word which
was "Dadda"
My dad was really helpful and helped me play football
And in 2015 a new family member was born;
My sister was born 20th May 2015,
And grew up loving the game Roblox.
Same as me but nowadays I play out
And play football games all day.

This is me... I am Aiden Leary and that is my life for now,
I've still got a while to go now.

Aiden Leary (12)
NET Red House Academy, Sunderland

Britain Loves To Hate Trains

The Class 142 Pacer is fast
Don't be so gullible, it only comes last
75mph don't be fooled by this bus on tracks

Due to the lack of wheel bogies, it bounces
It went over a bump and it started to dance
You could hear it screech before you saw it
It leapt forward uncontrollably

These are rarely in use
Most often when in preservation

My favourite train
Uses diesel like a crane

The waste from the lavatory went straight on the track
For the next train to go over it clickety clack.

Logan Morritt (13)
NET Red House Academy, Sunderland

I Am

This is about me
My hobbies are watching football
And to watch my favourite football team (Sunderland)
I also love to play football with friends
I love to put passion into playing football
And watching my team play
I will never forget the matches I went to
Like the one time we were playing Hull City
We were winning 4-3 but one of our players conceded
a penalty
They scored but to this day, I will respect our loss
I will never doubt my favourite football team
These are the bricks that built me.

Jake Cockton (11)
NET Red House Academy, Sunderland

My Dream Car

My car may not have gone far.
The age may surprise you.
It has 150bhp.
It is reliable.
It is unbeatable.

My car is a Honda.
It took no time to ponder.
It may not beat Supercars
But it is my freedom.
It is a future classic.

My car is a Civic Type R.
Its speedometer goes to 130.
It is beautiful.
It suits my cool style.

It keeps its value.
It is so fast.
It will cast
A smile on my face.
Every time I drive it.

This is my dream car.

Michael Jordan (13)
NET Red House Academy, Sunderland

Football Legend

It all starts with me watching football matches
At the age of seven, with my dad
Celebrating when Manchester City scored a goal
Against Manchester United
One-nil at the eighty-seventh minute
And then I knew
Manchester City is my dream club
There is one player that I like the most
Which is Kevin De Bruyne
The thing I like about him
Is his free kicks which go in all the time
He inspired me to become a football legend
That will play in Manchester City
And win many trophies for them.

David Ladipo (12)
NET Red House Academy, Sunderland

Family Travels

Before I leave the house
My family packs their bags
Off we go!
The smell of the airport reaches my nose
My mam and dad's voices fill with excitement as
we reach the gate
Finally on the plane
I strap in my seatbelt
The clouds look like candyfloss
The flight attendants spoke as they give my meal
I'm so excited to land!
My mam has her cup of coffee just before we land
Here at last
I get my suitcase
I go to my hotel
Unpack
And I can finally chill at the pool!

Isla Jackson (11)
NET Red House Academy, Sunderland

Football

As I walked onto the pitch
Anxiety filled my mind
Are we going to lose?
Will I get hurt?
As we warm up
Those thoughts come in one ear
And go out the other
As I walked onto the pitch
I was still nervous
The whistle blew
As we charged at the other players
The ball went up in the air...
Five minutes later
The ball was in the back of the net
We were screaming like men at the stadium
It was wild
We were running all over
Screaming and shouting.

Lucas Jarvis (11)
NET Red House Academy, Sunderland

My Family

Support, love and advice all come from my family
Forever forgiving, we rely upon one another
My brothers protect and look after me
I'm forever proud of the boys they became and
wanted to be
They never let me down in the thirteen years they
have known me
My mother, my very best friend, has never doubted me
She has watched her children grow, never leaving them
We love her lots which helped me become me
My family is everything to me
They make me be the best me.

Rebecca Ellison (13)
NET Red House Academy, Sunderland

Football, We Love It

Football, the bricks that built me.
Crowds chant in excitement as their team kicks the
ball that makes the sport.
Pieces of grass fly into the air,
As the players take a shot on goal.
Clubs coming face to face with each other in friendlies
and derbies,
Battling for the win.
Legends like Lionel Messi and Cristiano Ronaldo, who
are retiring soon,
The end of our footballing generation.
But soon, very soon, we will have new legends,
And that is football.

Jack Eagling (11)
NET Red House Academy, Sunderland

Me And My Doggy

Me and my dog in a field far away,
And the dog jumped so far it is a superstar.
The dog is a God and the God is the day.
The dog is as fast as a deity,
And my lion speed can't beat her.
With the ball flying through the field,
Me and my dog went flying over the field after.
After the dog was so tired,
We went back in a tyre.
The next day we went back,
And the ball is coming back.
The dog jumped up and caught the ball,
Just like a superstar.

Owen Sheldon (13)
NET Red House Academy, Sunderland

Destination Mexico

Waking up on a plane.
In the bright blue sky.
Birds flying past the aeroplane.
A smooth landing, sliding along the floor.

I step out of the plane.
Hot air swifts past me.
Brushing my hair in place.
The big hotel, with lots of rooms.
Sitting by the pool.
Trying new foods.
In my dream destination, Mexico!

In February, my dream will come true.
Excitement, anticipation, joy.
Which destination will be next?

Lena Pawlowska (12)
NET Red House Academy, Sunderland

Riley Moto Life

With the wind in my face,
I love to give chase,
My motorbike is green and shiny...
I clean him every day!

He is in my shed, safely stored,
I take him out when I am bored,
I ride it past my secondary school,
To the quarry, where I fly in the sky!
I feel as free as a bird.

Motocross is my ambition,
For this, I am very driven!
I hope to win a lot of awards,
And then my goal I will move towards!

Riley Naugher (11)
NET Red House Academy, Sunderland

Dance

Dance isn't just a sport
Dance is my life
Deep down in my core, I am dance
Dance is my passion.

Enthusiastic dancers cheer
I wait in fear
Nervously, I shiver
Wondering if I will be the winner
I step onto the floor
Judges smile, so I smile some more.

Behind every first place
Behind every outstanding costume
Behind every trophy
Is a beginner, trying their hardest.

Lacey McCully (12)
NET Red House Academy, Sunderland

The Lads In Red And White

Sunderland AFC is a labour of love.
Sometimes we win, sometimes we lose.
But I prefer it when we win.
Every week, it is as if our players are different people.

The Stadium of Light is a background.
While the electric atmosphere is cheering, on come
the lads in red and white.
Then, when we win, the spark in the club is reborn.
Until next week when we get battered 3-0 by Birmingham.

Oliver Rose (12)
NET Red House Academy, Sunderland

This Is Me

These are the bricks that built me,
My mum taught me to be a hard worker and
enjoy everything,
My stepdad showed me to never give up,
And my nana taught me to be kind.
I am made of kindness, happiness, and fun.
My walls are solid, I take shelter under my mum.
At my core, you will find a little sparkle of light
that never goes out.
I am Kai Nichols.

Kai (11)
NET Red House Academy, Sunderland

This Is Me

These are the bricks that built me,
I'm happy, my mum and dad help me if I need it.
I have the best pet and friends in the world.
My mum and dad taught me to be kind to people as well.
My dad taught me how to build a fire and make a zipline.
My best Christmas ever is when I go to my nan's and
have a Christmas dinner and open my presents.

Fletcher Murphy (11)
NET Red House Academy, Sunderland

The Best Day

I woke up very excited
Not being able to wait
I got ready with my Sunderland top on
As I saw the tip of the Stadium of Light
All I could see was red and white ants
The second I stepped into the stadium, I got butterflies
The sound of chants
The sound of the away fans
The sound of the ball
The match started.

Jake Potts (11)
NET Red House Academy, Sunderland

The Gamer

15:30 it all begins
The lights go out and it's game time
The controller's glow is irresistible
It attaches to my hand like it's a part of me

The game is on and the team rises
The shine of the screen has my eyes hypnotised
The crowd's screaming fills my ears
As it is the beginning of the end.

Jamie Hourigan (12)
NET Red House Academy, Sunderland

Roaring Joy!

In my room alone,
Staring at the ceiling,
Scrolling through my phone,
Waiting for that feeling.

The feeling in which,
That brings you joy,
Like when you were a child,
Receiving a new toy.

But now this feeling has a different cause,
It's the sound of music,
And when it roars!

Chloe Phuprate (13)
NET Red House Academy, Sunderland

This Is Me

This is me a little girl
Who has friends to share
I always look nice
Am the kindest of all
You can't find someone like me anywhere
Til one day I realise I am the best
When I look back in time, I am frozen
I am stuck in the past
And waiting for the best
In the end, I realise I am the shortest.

Shalom Oyebanji (12)
NET Red House Academy, Sunderland

My Body

My body, my feelings can't push the hate away,
Just follow and follow every day likes and likes on my post
They will never know the true me
Though I hated my body until I talked to my mum
She said, "You're beautiful and you should love your body"
So remember to love yourself and your body too.

Romany Cruddas (11)
NET Red House Academy, Sunderland

Feelings

I'm mad, I'm glad, I'm sad, I'm rad.
All of these feelings consume me.
Like a roundabout, they spin around waiting for a turn.
Feelings are powerful and I'm powerless.
Without them, I am numb.
I'm mad, I'm glad, I'm sad, I'm rad and I'm more
powerful than I think.

Jessica Fenwick (12)
NET Red House Academy, Sunderland

Miley's Family And Pets

Rigby is black, white and grey
He is the love of my life...
He is really naughty and he gets jealous!
He hates getting washed
He hates my other cat
Rigby has brown eyes
Rigby is funny!
He is crazy and gets tired after.

Miley Middlemiss (12)
NET Red House Academy, Sunderland

My Brain

I am disabled
But I am able
I may need help to do some things like you
Yet I can do more than you could ever do.

I have power
But you can't see it
Nor feel its presence
But in the end, I am disabled.

Vincent Gowland (12)
NET Red House Academy, Sunderland

This Is Me

These are the bricks that built me.
Logan P taught me how to defend myself,
Fletcher taught me how to enjoy life,
Gracie taught me my sense of humour,
These are my best friends,
I'm Usha.

Usha Quinn (11)
NET Red House Academy, Sunderland

This Is Me

This is me!

I am...
Cool
Smart

I am...
Asthmatic
Young

I love...
Cats
Food
My bed

I am Eden.

Eden Lilli Sampson (13)
NET Red House Academy, Sunderland

Me Kind

Me nice
Me kind
Me helpful
Me creative
Me a boy
Me a brother
Me is ginger
I am Johnjoe.

Johnjoe McKennell (13)
NET Red House Academy, Sunderland

This Is Me!

This is me, I am kind and caring,
This is me, I am friendly and supportive,
This is me, I am hardworking and lovely,
This is me, I am strong and intelligent.

This is me, I like football and shopping,
This is me, I don't like broccoli and Stoke City,
This is me, I like J.D. and McDonald's,
This is me, I don't like doing homework and drawing.

This is me, I have dark brown hair and green eyes,
This is me, I wear glasses and I'm tall,
This is me, I have olive skin and freckles,
This is me, I have some spots and a big forehead.

This is me, and I'm proud of it,
I am who I am and no one can change that,
You are who you are!
This is me!

Maisie Lowe (11)
Ormiston Horizon Academy, Tunstall

Charlotte Henshall

C aleb is my lover.

H amthra is one of my best friends.

A rchery is one of my hobbies.

R uby is one of my friends.

L ottie is an awesome friend.

O n Fridays, I do Scouts.

T aylor is a close friend.

T he thing I want to do most is be a palaeontologist.

E bonie is a wonderful friend.

H arshyan is a great friend.

E nding of my day can be great.

N etball is a hobby of mine.

S hooting is a thing I do in Scouts.

H appiness can be beautiful.

A t the end of the day, I am kind.

L ots of the time I play with friends.

L astly, I like acting and I am a dog person.

Charlotte Henshall (12)
Ormiston Horizon Academy, Tunstall

Reset, Beginning

Life is like a loop,
But it's always different,
My loop for example,
Is wake up, school, home,
Anime, games and sleep,
Reset.

Every time Saturday and Sunday comes,
It breaks because Friday,
Unlike the other days,
Ends in beginning.

Wake up, school, home,
Anime, games and sleep,
Beginning Saturday,
Wake up, games, anime,
Sleep and then,
Reset.

Life is a loop,
But it's always different,
And I think it's time,
To change it.

Life is boring,
If it's the same,
So live,

Life is a loop,
And it's your time,
To break through.

Troy Campbell (11)
Ormiston Horizon Academy, Tunstall

My Life From Four To Five

My name is Elizabeth and here is my life from age four,
If you enjoy crazy stories,
Then read this for some more,
Warning! Grab tissues and get ready,
I started to learn how to swim at age three,
When I was four years old, I actually had a dad,
But one day I was sadly told,
That he would never return because he was dead,
My mum bought me a cat called Luna and I loved her,
I was five when I started nursery,
Kids noticed that my dad wasn't around,
One day I just said, "He's dead!" to a ball called Mercury,
Then I was known as the girl with no dad,
Then my mum got me a dog called Pipper, who I adore.

Elizabeth May Walley (11)
Ormiston Horizon Academy, Tunstall

The Missing Piece

Puzzles come in different shapes and sizes,
Some big, some small, some long, some short,
Some complex with no resolve,
But the best one of all is the one that is yours.

The puzzle only you have,
Yet there's always one missing piece,
The little imperfection,
After all, we all have one.

Mine is when in May 2022 my dog (Molly) died,
And it left a piercing hole,
A piece that was irreplaceable,
That could never be rectified.

However, the puzzle can be pulled together again,
After all, if the piece is gone,
You need to accept that where it was, was there,
And will be there forever.

Lucas Austin-Broomhall (12)
Ormiston Horizon Academy, Tunstall

My Room

My room,
I love my room,
My room is part of me,
A part of my life,
A part of me.

I love decorating it,
Putting artwork on the walls,
Putting old photos of my family on the walls,
I love decorating my room,
My room.

I love my room,
It's a part of me,
A part of my life,
A part of me,
My room.

I love organising it,
Organising it the way I want,
Making it look clean,
My room,
I love organising my room,
My room.

I love my room,
It's a part of me

A part of my life,
A part of me,
My room.

Chelsea Ferris (11)
Ormiston Horizon Academy, Tunstall

What Defines Me

Although I'm a human just like you.
I am completely different and you are too.
But it's okay, you may not think so.
However, you are great, you just need to think, though.
We all have eyes, a body and a nose.
Although what's inside is a different better story.
Shining like a rose.
We can be described by words.
But they don't define us, nothing does really.
Apart from ourselves!
I may not know you and who you are.
I do know one thing however, you are you.
Amazing, bright and beautiful.
Just like the butterflies.
In your mind, by your side, all of the time.

Lola Mason (12)

Ormiston Horizon Academy, Tunstall

Bored

Tick-tock, tick-tock,
I stare, mind blank, at the very hand in front of me,
Tick tock, tick-tock.
A pencil snaps, pens click, paper tears,
Teacher glances, here and there but I frown,
Dull as slate, my mind in a frantic state,
A mark so low I anticipate,
Tick-tock, tick-tock.
For boredom I now wish,
Forever it seems,
Mind branded the mask of fear,
A cry or scream naught but a single tear as dark falls
around,
Tick-tock, tick-tock.
Bell shatters silence,
But I don't notice,
For now, again mind blank as slate,
I hand in my test,
Tick-tock, tick-tock.

Benjamin Burrows (12)
Ormiston Horizon Academy, Tunstall

Family

Family is something you need to have
Something that is deep within your heart
Doesn't have to be blood related
As long as you are there

You may not feel you are wanted
But deep down just think
They will always be there for you
As long as you are there

People may be mean
But you're not the only one out there
Your family loves you with all their heart
As long as you are there

Nobody knows until you tell them
You don't have to keep anything a secret
Family is family
Nothing will change that
As long as you are there.

Isabella Allcock (12)
Ormiston Horizon Academy, Tunstall

Ego

Having an ego can be great yet it could also be a weight
If it is treated right, then it won't fight.
Your ego can go up and down.
Create a smile or a frown.
But remember a frown can go upside down.
With enough negativity, it can sting like a bee.
But positivity can set you free.
A monster on your shoulder can grow and grow.
If fed with mean words, it won't let go.
The beast finds these like we find treats.
Oh yes, it's just like a feast.
To overcome the beast you must.
Find a person you trust.
They'll help you believe so you can achieve.

Liam Twardochleb (12)
Ormiston Horizon Academy, Tunstall

My Life At Its Finest

When I was born,
I knew that the time had come,
To have some fun,
The first thought in my head.

Strength, confidence and happiness,
As my personality grows,
Bigger and bigger.

As I sing the sweet tune,
I call my life,
I hear my phone go *ding*,
To the right.

My friends, a highlight of my life,
Lovely, kind and funny,
My friends as sweet as honey.

My family give me a shield of comfort,
They are forever in my heart,
They forever give me joy,
And will forever bring happiness.

Hannelore Makamure (11)
Ormiston Horizon Academy, Tunstall

This Is Me

These are the bricks that built me
Never going to crumple it down
Just add on for my family
Friends always there to comfort me
I keep on building it on
Soon, it will be built for the future
I have a promise I have to learn to keep
I have to keep bright just like blue
Do you like the colour too?
Also never giving up for the future I want
Love cars and love restoring them
I promised my dad to assist him to do it
The family I love mean the world
The school is on the side.

Deacon Grocott (12)
Ormiston Horizon Academy, Tunstall

Myself (I Am)

My name is Marvelous Samuel, I was born in the month of
March
I am ambitious and I want to be a police officer
I am responsible, respectful and resilient
I am not violent, I am exactly the opposite
I am empathetic, loving and caring
I like my family, friends and life
I look forward to my future ambitions
My hobbies are football and games
I am used to playing football and I am a great defender
I am sincere, sharing and courageous.

Marvelous Samuel (11)

Ormiston Horizon Academy, Tunstall

Friends

My friends are my height,
My friends are my age,
But I fit in
Just right.

My energy doesn't match,
Neither does my name,
But no matter what,
We're all the same.

But we are not the same,
We are in fact different
We don't have the same hair
We don't have the same anything.

But at the end of the day
We're only ten minutes away
We are all friends
Just friends.

Damien Oliveira (13)
Ormiston Horizon Academy, Tunstall

What Makes Me, Me?

There's a lot of things that make me, me,
But here are just a few.
I'm shy,
But if you get to know me, I am loyal.
I want to be an author,
Writing gives me joy.
I like to play video games,
Mobile and console.
I've loved superheroes,
For as long as I can remember.
Otters are the best,
At least according to me.
No one in the world is just like me,
But that's what makes us all unique.

Sophia Lowe (11)
Ormiston Horizon Academy, Tunstall

Daily Life

I am 12 years old and I have one sister
And I have two pet rabbits.
One of them is 18 weeks and the other I don't know
But all I know is that they like to eat and sleep
The sports I like are football, rugby and dodgeball
On a daily basis, I go to school, come back and change
Then I eat, then homework, then TV.
Then make rabbit food and clean the litter tray.
Then I go on my bike, then shower and sleep.

Zedekiah Nasau
Ormiston Horizon Academy, Tunstall

Me And My Silence

I just sit there, with my silence,
Never speak, never a peep,
I don't speak or do,
I want to,
I just sit there dreaming.

I get taken for being cold,
But maybe I'm not bold,
Maybe I want to speak,
But stay with my silence,
Never making a peep.

You may think I don't like you,
But don't take me wrong,
I like to stay with my silence,
Never letting it go.

Emilia Niedzwiecka (12)
Ormiston Horizon Academy, Tunstall

Depression

I blamed my past,
I blamed my school,
I blamed everything, until no more.

The thoughts to keep quiet could only keep me safe.
The only thing that calmed me.
From losing friends to being called names,
I could no longer take.

From Monday to Friday,
I started to look for therapists,
But of course, no one helped.
And let me tell you it's hard.
There's no right fit.

Niámh Challinor (12)
Ormiston Horizon Academy, Tunstall

I Love Basketball

B y my side will be Steph Curry.

A chieving slowly in my mind.

S omeday, it will come true.

K nowledge of basketball.

E very day, non-stop practising.

T he day is gonna happen.

B asketball is my favourite sport.

A ll I think about.

L osing but winning.

L earning about basketball now I'm in the National League.

Harvey Johnson (12)
Ormiston Horizon Academy, Tunstall

Marvellous Music!

Music is my favourite thing,
There are so many different genres,
It makes me so joyful,
It is so super fantastic.

There is K-pop that I love,
The girl groups are enjoyable,
Especially New Jeans,
Hanni is my bias.

It is such a comfort,
It keeps me entertained,
I will never stop listening to it,
No matter what.

Aniela Niedzwiecka (11)
Ormiston Horizon Academy, Tunstall

About Me

O livia is my half-sister.
L iv is my nickname.
I have brown hair.
V ery straight and long hair.
I am getting braces soon.
A m I ready for a change?

M y dream is to own a business.
A n ambitious job of selling beauty products.
E very day I try my best.

Olivia-Mae Robinson (13)
Ormiston Horizon Academy, Tunstall

Family

My family, of whom there are many,
Are always supporting me when achieving things
Positive and negative my family are
But some might say bizarre
Loving and kind actions are always in their mind
As they care for people in poverty and for the lonely
I love my family and they love me
For they care and are always with me.

Paul Quminakelo (13)
Ormiston Horizon Academy, Tunstall

Me

This is me, I'm 11 years old
But I'm not very bold
My favourite colour is yellow
My least favourite food is marshmallow
My favourite animal is a panda which I adore
I already have 7, I hope to have more
The things I don't like make me feel it's not right
But the things I do may be different to you.

Olivia Partridge (11)

Ormiston Horizon Academy, Tunstall

What Makes Me, Me

C   olouring is my favourite hobby
H   appy and cheerful all the time
A   mazing at everything I do
R   espectful and polite
L   oves to play with animals
I   ntelligent and has a spark of wonder
E   ntertaining and full of laughter.

Charlie Koajan (11)
Ormiston Horizon Academy, Tunstall

My Name

E motional.
V ery kind.
I 'm 11 years old.
E vie.

H appy.
O verjoyed.
L azy.
D ancer.
C urious.
R ight-handed.
O blivious.
F unny.
T all.

Evie Holdcroft (11)
Ormiston Horizon Academy, Tunstall

Death

D o people always have to die?
E verybody does eventually but they are never forgotten
A lthough we don't like it, it has to happen
T hinking about who we have lost every day
H eaven has a special place for all of our loved ones.

Hollie Bloor (13)
Ormiston Horizon Academy, Tunstall

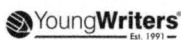

This Is Me

C aring and kind

O bvious

O wner of many friends and things

P lays football a lot at school

E nergetic and always moving

R eads all the time in bed and the school library.

W inner of things.

Cooper Williamson (12)

Ormiston Horizon Academy, Tunstall

Summer Is The Best Time Of Year

Summer is the best time of year
Sunshine, rainbows, lollipops
Summer, it's the best time of year
Sit down, lie down, do not frown
Summer is the best time of year
Lay off school, do not fear because
Summer is the best time of year.

Nathan Walker (12)
Ormiston Horizon Academy, Tunstall

This Is Me

B is for brilliant
E is for excellent
N is for not good at art
J is for Jackson
A is for amazing
M is for marvellous
I is for intelligent
N is for nice.

Benjamin Robert Jackson (11)

Ormiston Horizon Academy, Tunstall

Dancing Tips

D azzling to the eyes
A mazing exercise
N ot for everyone
C an't always be correct
I ndependent all the time
N ot everyone will get it first try
G lamourous hobby.

Zac Jones (11)
Ormiston Horizon Academy, Tunstall

All About Me

I watch Stoke City lose every week
I like canoeing and I sometimes watch cricket
I play football with my dad in the back garden
I want to become a goalkeeper
My favourite football player is Jack Butland.

Kian Hall (11)
Ormiston Horizon Academy, Tunstall

The Things In My Life

My name is Saleh,
I like most sports but I don't wear shorts,
I have a brother named Yusuf and a sister too,
Her name is Ameerah,
I am a Muslim,
I try to be smart to the end of my whim.

Saleh Maqsood (12)
Ormiston Horizon Academy, Tunstall

Music

M y name is Wiki
U sed to listen to pop music
S inging is really cool
I am sarcastic, loud and really cool
C oke is yummy and the best drink.

Wiki Krzus (11)

Ormiston Horizon Academy, Tunstall

McKenzie

M y family
C aring
K ind
E at
N o football makes me sad
Z ebras
I ce
E nvy.

McKenzie Birch (12)
Ormiston Horizon Academy, Tunstall

This Is Me

E nergetic enough to do anything.
V ery good at games
A lways go outside with my mates
N ever will play on a console.

Evan Wood (11)

Ormiston Horizon Academy, Tunstall

This Is Me

L ikes football
O ver boundaries
U ses calculator in maths
I s not naughty
S hocking at eating fast.

Louis Jones (11)
Ormiston Horizon Academy, Tunstall

This Is Me

E llie is smelly

L oyal

L oving towards family and friends

I ndependent

E nergetic and crazy.

Ellie Mae Ashby (11)
Ormiston Horizon Academy, Tunstall

About Me!

A mazing and kind
L oving and more
F un all the time
I nteresting
E ntertaining when bored.

Alfie Winter (11)
Ormiston Horizon Academy, Tunstall

Lucas

L oyal Lucas.
U nderstanding Lucas.
C reative Lucas.
A mazing Lucas.
S uper Lucas.

Lucas Beardmore (11)
Ormiston Horizon Academy, Tunstall

This Is Me

I am kind
I have a beautiful mind
When I put the work in
I know I can do anything
My smile always shines
I love to rhyme
My mum says I bring joy
My dad says I should have been a boy
My nana says I am the best
My grandad says I am a treasure
I am not a pest
I always do well on tests
I am a good friend and will be there in
your darkest moments
I will always try my best and I will try to succeed
I will never let my family down
I will always make them proud
I am proud of me
I am proud of you
No matter what happens
As long as you are kind
I will always stick up for you.

Millie Hunt (11)
Outwood Academy Bydales, Marske-By-The-Sea

This Is Me

Blazing blue as the roaring sea,
The eyes, *my* eyes that belong to *me*.
Golden hair that hangs down loose,
I wish I could fly like a silvery goose.
Fierce and enduring like a leopard in the snow,
Fierce and enduring like the winds that blow.
Intelligent and studious like an amber-eyed owl,
I listen to the wolves that howl,
Without fear.

I am confident and kind,
I have a very talented mind.
I am beautiful; you are too.
Like the blossoms that grow,
Through frost and snow.
We will go on!

Lucy Aditi Long (11)
Outwood Academy Bydales, Marske-By-The-Sea

This Is Me

These are the bricks that built me,
Sometimes it's not so easy to see,
Kind of introverted I may appear,
But when you meet me, I'll annoy you, my peer,
My ginger hair
Is quite a scare,
Addicted to my laptop screen,
Half the time I'm nowhere to be seen,
In love with my bed,
It's kinda sad to be said,
Always caring,
You will be surprised by me, not at our first meeting.

Amelia Holland (11)
Outwood Academy Bydales, Marske-By-The-Sea

Tired Of Being Told

I'm tired of being told that being stubborn is bad,
What's wrong with knowing my worth?
They say I should comply because it is their word
against mine,
Is being me so wrong?

I'm tired of being told that being competitive is bad,
What's wrong with wanting to succeed?
They say I should be a 'team player' and enjoy taking part,
Is being me so wrong?

I'm tired of being told that having opinions is bad,
What's so wrong with thinking for myself?
They say we should express ourselves and be our own
person until we really do it,
Is being me so wrong?

I'm tired of being told being intelligent is bad,
What's wrong with excelling in the world?
I go to school for all these hours but being better
is now bad,
Is being me so wrong?

But now I've changed
I'm no longer me but instead who you want me to be,
I'm tired of being quiet,

Doubtful and dull,
Is being the same so fun?

I wish someone would give me a rest but to them what
I want is not the best,

I'm tired of being told who I am, I am me.

Georgia Weeks
Preston School Academy, Yeovil

Poles

I can feel the way they look at me,
Frowning down, in disbelief
They play games at guessing
Which country I am from, village, district?

I over-achieve to make up for it,
Would get a PhD, a doctorate,
Anything at all to make me an equal
To kids with normal surnames, kids from Britain.

I smile and laugh, wanting to cry,
As they make fun of my country's dishes,
Asking me to say this, that and the other,
I oblige. They smile and laugh.

It's hard to explain.
I was born here, I can live here,
And yet I will never belong.
I'm not an immigrant, I think.

I confuse everyone I meet,
I behave in lessons, grade 9's expectations,
I try so hard. I get so tired, all for recognition,
They do not even try to pronounce Kusmierczyk.

I can feel the way they look at me,
Frowning down in disbelief
When I try to tell them rather than ignore
That I'm not 'Stella K', not anymore.

Stella Kusmierczyk
Preston School Academy, Yeovil

Who Am I?

Who am I?
I'd tell you if I knew,
I hide in the shadows,
Like they don't have a clue.

What am I?
That's long overdue,
No one truly knows,
And that includes me too.

Who was I?
I was happy and new,
Free of sorrow,
That much is true.

My parents are worried,
Because my friends had scurried,
Alone, once again
Me and my thoughts,
Left to run,
Like a notepad and pen.

Their words had left me black and blue,
The words hurting more,
And sticking like glue.

It's going to hurt for a while,
It'll make my mind run an extra mile,

But I'll be better,
I'll become tough.
I'll know who I am,
And that's enough.

Izzy Hall
Preston School Academy, Yeovil

Fungi

At my core, you will find,
No peace of mind,
A very big worry,
A want to sorry,
A sadness growing like a fungi,
That is why I am not a fun guy,

A sea of sorrow running over me,
My warmth left like a winter tree,
An urge to say sorry for what I have done,
But no words come out like they are held in with a gun,
A sadness growing like a fungi,
That is why I am not a fun guy,

Depression hits me like a tsunami,
No happiness runs through me,
That is not me,
I am fun and kind,
Like I have a lovely mind,

I have good friends,
With a happiness that will never end,
A happiness growing like a fungi,
That is why I am a fun guy.

Oliver Finch
Preston School Academy, Yeovil

The Life Of An Addict

I walk down the street as car brakes screech,
The hiss of smoke and the jeering of drivers,
Fills my ears as they become dividers.

A sign to tell me that I don't fit in,
While I walk down an alley lean into a bin,
The hateful sniggers of everyone else continue
to tell me I shouldn't exist.

I weep at night in the cold lack of rooms,
Asleep in an alley,
The ugliest tunes.

Need only a warm place to live,
A house or a shelter to let me live fully,
I pray to you all don't assume that I can escape
on my own.

I need your help to exit,
This dangerous cycle of the psyche,
Please bring attention to addicts.

Nathan Yell (13)
Preston School Academy, Yeovil

All In A Cup

I love the outside,
The fresh air the sun,
With my foot dying to kick,
My legs like to run.

I do not love writing,
My handwriting is not the best,
But I am really quite intelligent,
I do very well in my tests.

Snakes and spiders can make me queasy,
I would still hold them if nobody else would,
I find I love racing,
I would always beat you running up a hill.

Back at my lovely warm house,
I have got a little sister,
Who I love dearly,
But she is really loud, I have never heard her whisper.

If you put them all together,
Mix and mash them up,
And then you get me,
All in a cup.

Seb Farwell

Preston School Academy, Yeovil

Keira Boyd

K ind is what I want to be,
E very day though, slips away from me.
I want to achieve in all I do,
R ight now, I dream through and through.
A nd all that matters are my family's joys,

B right and wonderful childhood toys.
O bviously, each young memory paved my path,
Y es, we all forgot those childhood laughs.
D ays slip away from us all though,

I always try to reach up high so
S omeday I can reach my dream,

M y goal is to be on that stage and gleam.
E very day to be one step closer to where I want to be.

Keira Boyd (14)
Preston School Academy, Yeovil

No One Cares

The truth about this world,
No one cares.
No one cares about you,
You and your ambitions or hopes.
No one cares about
Fears or beliefs.
No one cares about
You and your likes or sorrows.
No one cares.
People don't care about what matters,
And what makes you, you.
They only care about the outside not in,
The inside is the only thing that truly matters.
And as long as you are true to yourself
That is what matters.
Not the appearance but the personality
And speaking from the heart
That is what truly matters.
Not popularity, personality.

Rufus Suter (12)
Preston School Academy, Yeovil

If I Had Wings

If I had wings
I would touch the body of the rainbow
And glide on the sand's breath.

If I had wings
I would taste the mouthful of a moonbow
As cold as icy glaciers.

If I had wings
I would listen to the crescent of the moon
Tiptoeing over the Indian Ocean.

If I had wings
I would breathe heavily
And drink the smell of sand drops.

If I had wings
I would stare at the northern lights
As it transfers into spontaneous shapes.

If I had wings
I would dream
Of jumping the oceans
And swimming in the canyons.

William Flynn (12)
Preston School Academy, Yeovil

This Is Me

I can hide in a corner,
And hide from the world,
But sometimes I feel welcome,
And come out to stir,

A task can seem too mighty,
And I hide away in fear,
But I can give it a go,
And throw away my tears,

My body may look different,
Dressed up in old clothes,
And my hair is a different colour,
With a pair of glasses on my nose,

But in the chaos,
Other people are not the same,
Because I am different,
I am strange.

Thomas Pratt (12)
Preston School Academy, Yeovil

Find Me

With so many giants,
You may not hear my squeak,
One of eight billion,
Yet I am unique.

I may not be helpful,
I may not be strong,
I'm not the sharpest,
But my story is long.

It may be hard to see me,
Try to break past my disguise,
It may be hard to read me,
If you don't get past all the lies.

I'm not the best,
I'm not the worst,
I won't come last,
But I'm never first.

Even if you see me,
I'm not the best I can be,
You might think I am special,
Just try and find me!

Michael Appleby
Preston School Academy, Yeovil

This Is Me

These are the bricks that built me,
I may be shy,
But I can not lie,
Dancing is a part of me,
Feeling proud and free,
Friends are the ones that help me,
Overcome my fears,
I'm not just made out of sticks and stones,
Bullying can really hurt,
Some may think as I'm boring as can be,
But wait until they see the other side of me,
Make-up and dance, what wonder it gives,
Just wait until I'm up there,
And you're down there.

Izabella Atkins (12)
Preston School Academy, Yeovil

This Is Me

My name is Noah Downes,
I rarely show a frown.
I'm usually a happy chappy, and I am always
incredibly happy.
I love football and have been obsessed with it
since I could crawl.
I shoot with accuracy,
I defend with power
and play football
hour after hour.
My family are cool
and together we rule.
We enjoy the beach,
music and walking,
but most of all,
we enjoy talking.
This is my poem
And this is *me!*

Noah Downes (12)
Preston School Academy, Yeovil

Danny

I am Egyptian by birth and descent,
I live in the United Kingdom at present.
I am short and dark-haired,
I can be both prepared and unprepared.
I like to read, play on my phone,
And I like to swim, cycle and eat ice cream cones.

I am from a family of four,
Kind but strict parents, and one more.
An obnoxious brother, David his name,
Annoying and accompanying me is his game.

I am made of intelligence, jokes and good cheer,
And a dash of eccentricity;
Put them together
And you get me!

Danny Aziz (11)
Preston School Academy, Yeovil

The Gleam Of Gold

I have not scaled the ladder
I have not set the bar
I have not earned any trophies
I have not gotten far
So, I stare into the mirror
And judge myself too
Will I ever get better
I have no clue

I have not won awards
Or set the world right
But I will try my best
And I know I will be alright
So, I glare into the mirror
And cry so much too
But do not worry
It is nothing new.

Siobhan Geldenhuys (11)
Preston School Academy, Yeovil

What Makes Me, Me

I struggle to believe all of the things that make me, me
It's like when I'm sitting under a tree
And I think about all the stuff about me
I think about my eyes, my name
Or maybe even that I am a he
But I know mainly that it is my personality
But then I think that can't be it
I mean there can't just be one thing
And then it rings
That one thing is everything.

Harrison Ashfield (11)
Preston School Academy, Yeovil

This Is Me

I am a Ravenclaw,
With will,
And knowledge,
And creativity,

I am a Hufflepuff,
With loyalty,
And patience,
And honesty,

I am a Gryffindor,
With leadership,
And determination,
And bravery,

I am a Slytherin,
With ambition,
And imagination,
And pride.

Elizabeth Nielsen (11)
Preston School Academy, Yeovil

This Is Me

I am kind,
I am generous,
I am thoughtful,
This is me.

I play the piano,
I play badminton,
I play games,
This is me.

I hate spiders,
I hate losing,
I hate punishment,
This is me.

I am me,
Nobody can change this,
I am who I want to be,
This is me.

Thomas Hares (12)
Preston School Academy, Yeovil

I Am

I am my likes and opinions.
I am my smarts and habits.
I am funny and caring.
I am kind and love nature.
I am patient and like comedy.
I am a gamer who never gives up.
I am myself and my personality.
I am Lucas Foxwell, the strategic one.

Lucas Foxwell (11)
Preston School Academy, Yeovil

I'm Not A Girl Who Can't Fight, That Needs A Man Every Time

I might be shy but I won't let you expect me to be loud.
If you try to make me cry, I won't let it slide,
If you try to break my walls, you'll end up on the floor.
You might think I'm a heroine in a story,
But I'm really the real hero who can live on her own.
Little girls grow up with princesses same as me,
But I also hope one day a princess can be her own self.
There are loads of role models for girls,
But always depend on a man to save the day.
I just hope one day, just one quiet day,
That there is a new princess or role model for little girls.
When I have a little girl, she will be independent,
And don't need a man, who also stands her ground.
But let's hope one day people raise women,
Who can fight for something for what they stand their ground for.

Katelin Collins (13)
St Thomas Aquinas Secondary School, Glasgow

Who I Am

When I was young I loved playing with toys
Now that I am fourteen I am either out with my friends,
Or playing games on my Xbox or phone.
One thing I love more than games is listening to music
Or talking to my close friends.
Now that aside, I would like to talk about who made me,
My mum and dad, have been with me ever since I was born,
And will stick up for me no matter what.
My brother is also a big part of my life.
He is annoying but also helps me a lot.
I love Christmas and Halloween but birthdays are also good.
My birthday is the 13th of May and my middle name
is David.
I've grown up in Knightswood my whole life, as I have
never moved house.
I also have a Saint name which is Anthony,
So my full name is Owen David Anthony Baxter.

Owen Baxter (14)
St Thomas Aquinas Secondary School, Glasgow

This Is Me

These are the bricks that built me, competitive, protective, having friends and being part of a family.

You see I am an introvert and extrovert, a blend of both.
I am artistic, creative and intelligent, a perfect mix.

My base is more complex with deeper emotions like empathy and resilience.
I have a compassionate heart.
An open mind.

I am strong and proud, my roots run deep, my background is part of me.
As a black individual celebrating diversity.
I face diversity with strength and grace.

Anastasia Saki (14)
St Thomas Aquinas Secondary School, Glasgow

Energetic

Being energetic can be lots of joy and fun
But sometimes, it can be a pain in the bum.

I'm like a battery, sometimes I can feel down
Or sometimes I'm very chatty.

Sometimes my battery is full of energy
And I spread that energy
Or my battery feels empty
And I just want to be left alone.

I get charged up by being with my friends and
listening to music
And most importantly, my family.

Olivia Watt (13)
St Thomas Aquinas Secondary School, Glasgow

What It Means To Be Chinese Living In The UK

Doesn't matter where you're from,
No matter if you are African-born, American
born or European-born,
We are all equal,
As a Chinese with a UK citizen,
Can get pressurised,
Doesn't matter,
Be yourself,
Even though I am young,
A dream of engineering at my number one,
Hope to be successful,
Won't be dull.

Ivan Wang (14)
St Thomas Aquinas Secondary School, Glasgow

The Amazing Calvin

C is for Calvin, so caring day by day
A is for affectionate, and amazing in each way
L is for our laughter, your loyalty and love
V is for the very special one sent from above
I is for intelligent, incredible, ideal
N is for the nice way you always make us feel.

Calvin Stronach (14)
St Thomas Aquinas Secondary School, Glasgow

Stressed

Anxiety lives in my body when I'm out and in a big group
Comfort jumper or fuzzy socks help me at these times
People being loud or people screaming trigger this button
Big groups scare me, make me feel mad or
sometimes stressed
School gives me a lot of anxiety, especially in
certain subjects.

Maisie Morton (13)
St Thomas Aquinas Secondary School, Glasgow

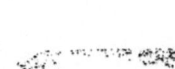

The Boy From Scotland

There once was a boy from Scotland.
Who loved to play in the rain.
One day he tripped.
And broke his hip.
Now he's in serious pain.

Calvin Stronach (14)
St Thomas Aquinas Secondary School, Glasgow

This Is Me

I live in a world full of wolves.
They bit and sneered and laughed and snarled.
They gather like thick fog under stormy clouds.
Fur black, like they have been painted by swaths
of smog and soot.

They bark and bite at birds and bugs.
Blend together as if they were one amorphous nightmare.
They roam through forests glided by light.
Its golden warmth reflects away, as though it had learned
the truth.

Somewhere else, faded among the autumn leaves, I
stand alone.
Distantly, shrieking howls sound off.
The sound echoes towards me and my dirt-stained,
ginger fur.
Making me flinch as if the dirt that hides me would
ever truly protect.

One day, they will find their next victim.
Only a fluffy little fledgeling, only a year young.
The ever-present tug in my chest burns fiercely again
and my vision warps.
As if the distance between us is stretching and wavering,
leaving me unable to help.

(As if that was ever what was stopping me.)

It happens slowly.

One day, we happen to be retreating from our common enemy.
When we blunder into each other.
Something new curls in my chest.
It's warm in a way the sunlight never quite could be.

After a while, the direct grime and guilt wash away.
Instead of black smog, my fur is sunshine itself.
A bright, meaning orange that casts a glow of its own upon us.
Their downy feathers have grown into the hallmarks of a true predator.

The sun shines on us, and together we listen for the howls that will never reach us again.

Neve Bentley (16)
The Read School, Drax

People

They are confusing animals,
There's no half-and-half thinking,
They're the only animals to overthink,
So many signals for the same thing.

Me being myself, I don't understand this animal,
Even though I am one of them,
This is because of my autism,
I find it difficult to understand those around me.

Even when we know humans are the most complex animals,
I find it overwhelming to try and understand them,
This leads me to meltdowns and shutdowns,
I panic, shut myself away and become a madman.

Back to people,
It can be fascinating to watch them communicate,
But not always understand the mixed signals,
It can also be fascinating to become their friends.

Once you become their friends, they can help you
understand the rules,
I know I like rules but not too many,
But I think that this is a fascinating creature that
makes up too many rules,
As long as I can take shortcuts, I am fine.

Not many people would understand,
Some people do understand, like my favourite teacher,
But many don't want to know others' struggles,
That's the world we live in!

Teddy Snowden (13)
The Read School, Drax

Don't Judge A Book By It's Cover: This Is Me

Sometimes I stare at people and wonder who they are,
Sometimes I stare and I think I know who they are
But that's just the beginning.

You might talk to them
You might try to know them better,
But estimating doesn't give you any evidence.

This is like when you see a pebble in the ocean,
This is like finding a wide and perfect stone for skimming,
But it's not until you pick it up that you see it's a chunky
heavy rock,
You could toss it away or think of all the advantages it has.

Imagine seeing a tiny twinkling light in the depths of the
ocean,
Imagine swimming towards it thinking it's a flounder fish,
Glistening in the sunlight,
It's not until you swim closer that it's a deep sea angler fish,
Preparing to bite your fingers off.

What you might see is a show-off diver,
Who is actually anxious to dive into the sea,
It's not about what you literally can see,
But when you dive beneath the surface,
You find their twinkling personalities.

Lucy Thompson (13)
The Read School, Drax

200

This Is Me! Christmas

The Christmas tree lights in the passing houses glow
Walking home, I'm freezing in the ice-cold snow
I purse my lips and feel the warmth of my tea
I wonder if Santa will bring presents for me?

Embarking on his journey, away from the North Pole
I truly hope he doesn't bring me any coal
I hear a giant clatter on my roof
I wonder if it could be a reindeer's hoof?

Downstairs, I hear a sudden bang and a cough
Something seems extremely off
I snuck downstairs, shocked to see who stood by the tree
I think it's Santa so I squeal with glee.

They turned around but I wasn't glad
Because the large man I saw was my dad
I guess Santa isn't real
But I am 30 so it's no big deal.

Grace Wilson (13)
The Read School, Drax

This Is Me

This is me,
Born in a snowstorm,
A beloved present under the Christmas tree,
With a massive and amazing family,

This is me,
On my first day of school,
With my big sisters wanting me to play it cool,

This is me,
Getting my first-ever sports award,
On my highest shelf, it would be stored,

This is me,
On my last day of university,
Education sure did feel like an eternity,

This is me,
At my first-ever job,
It isn't high paying but it is good enough,

This is me on my wedding day,
So many friends and family,
I am glad I didn't have to pay,

This is me,
At retirement,
Enjoying freedom from work and that 6 am alarm
is no longer a requirement,

This is me,
At the end of my life,
With a massive and amazing family,
Oh, how brilliant my life has been,
Everything that I ever wanted it to be.

Malachi Riley (12)
The Read School, Drax

All About Me

When I was born, I had a brother,
He made my mum a mother,
I love my family dearly,
They help me learn clearly.

I have the best, best, best, best friends ever,
Some even say I'm clever,
I am a very sporty girl,
Who likes to eat a Twirl.

I have a cute cockapoo called Charlie,
His fur is the colour of barley,
He makes me proud,
And looks like a cloud.

When I am older I want to be a teacher,
I hope I won't be a preacher,
I really hope you don't think my poem is lame,
But who knows when we will meet again?

Libby Sturdivant (12)
Thetford Grammar School, Thetford

This Is Me

I eat food, then eat more,
So much so, it could be food galore,
I'm good at sports and great at running,
A leap, a jump, and I'm at Airsoft, gunning.

I make weird noises, such as woof and neigh,
I'm amazing in ways and I glow like a sunray,
I'm sweet, I'm salty,
I'm never really faulty.

I'm deceiving yet truthful, I lie and I'm good,
I'm sporty and smart, but stupidly silly,
I'm happy, I'm friendly, though I can be quite naughty,
This is me.

Callum McLoughlin (12)
Thetford Grammar School, Thetford

Who Am I?

Fun-sharer
Hockey player
Music lover
Honey hugger
Video game player
Who am I?

As happy as can be
As tall as a tree
As buzzed as a bee
Energetic as a cheetah
Pure as I want to be
Who am I?

Through the mist and the breeze
I fly through the trees
In the sky where I fly
I realise something

I'm all these things mixed together
This will be me forever
Happy or sad
I'm glad who I am
This is me!

Olivia Cradock (11)
Thetford Grammar School, Thetford

This Is Me

T	he best season is autumn
H	alloween and pumpkin spice are my favourite; they are so nice
I	like going out on walks with my dog
S	mells of cinnamon and pumpkin spice make the autumn season so nice

I	n the air are leaves blowing around
S	chool is over for two weeks. Time for some treats

M	y garden plants turn brown and orange
E	eek, Halloween is here, time for more and more treats.

Willow Goldson (11)
Thetford Grammar School, Thetford

What I Love

I love parrots
I love little dogs
I adore chickens
I adore cats
I hate big dogs

I love nature
I love trees
I adore long walks
I adore good beats

I love the crunch of the leaves
I love the autumnal breeze
I adore spring
I adore singing
I hate loudness
I hate darkness.

Sebastian Metcalf (11)
Thetford Grammar School, Thetford

This Is Me

My name is Ashton,
I like to play games,
Slowly going by with the days.

Although I am an academic,
I leave behind my relic.
A soft and slow ship,
Rising very quick.

Somedays I am sick,
Although others start with a kick.
Science is part of me,
I wonder what I will grow up to be.

Ashton Green (12)
Thetford Grammar School, Thetford

This Is Me!

T his is me,
H opefully, a future author,
I try my hardest to be kind,
S wimming is my favourite sport.

I n my own world, inside my head,
S ophie is my name.

M y bookshelf is piled high with books,
E njoying the life I live!

Sophie Codd (11)
Thetford Grammar School, Thetford

This Is Me

Dangerous, daring,
Sailing gives me the rush,
But my mum gives me the shush.

Rugby makes me strong,
Football makes me bored,
Cricket makes me quick,
But hockey makes me sick.

Athletics makes me cower,
100 metres makes me tower.

Brian Morse (11)
Thetford Grammar School, Thetford

This Is Me

G reat at playing games
E pic at being clumsy
O rganising, I'm trying to achieve
R emembering things is not my thing
G ood at sportsmanship
E agle eyes all the time.

George Bullen (11)
Thetford Grammar School, Thetford

Waste Of Nature

Walking down the road at dusk there's nothing you can't see,
But all I saw were hedgehogs trying to flee,
They never make it to the ditch,
That evening, I thought it could have been a witch,
Not knowing what to do,
I made a plan to stop people revving their load,
That morning, I put a sign up,
I was hoping that I would maybe have some luck,
The following day, I went out to see a dead fox and I was disgusted by the sight,
I was going to pick it up but I realised it had mites,
I thought to myself I couldn't leave him there,
When I approached him, he gave me a wicked stare,
I kept walking down the road but no neighbours I could see,
I went inside to tell my mum and she said she's proud of me.

Elsa Buckland (12)
Wadham School, Crewkerne

That's Me

Down I gaze,
Into the clear blue, the frolicking waves,
A sea of a million crystals of aquamarine.
And I stare down into it...
And I watch it,
As the water dances, so happy, so free...
What do I see?
I see a girl,
Billowing, fiery hair,
Her eyes mirror the depths of the ocean.
I see a short, calm girl,
She has a family, siblings, two of them, and she's in the middle.
I see a pale face,
Cheeks blushed rose by the cold winds of Wales,
Freckled by sundrops,
A stout red-brown Dachshund by her side.
The waves ripple,
Playfully splashing her little paws,
Chewing at the sand.
There we stand, as one,
A poppy in a field of daisies.
The grey-blue skies shroud us,
Like a blanket stitched with candyfloss clouds.

The sea like a magic mirror,
What's that I see?
That's me.

Poppy Hale (11)
Wadham School, Crewkerne

Who I Am

I am an eleven-year-old girl,
Who hates reading, but writes books,
I love animals, but hate spiders,
I love the summer but also love autumn,
I am a very anxious and quiet person who hates crowded places.
Once you get to know me, I am a funny person,
I love tulips and roses and love the vanilla scent,
I love playing and watching football,
My favourite time of year is Christmas,
I love my family, best friends and nephew,
When I am sad and want to be alone, music and rain make me happy.
My favourite letters are D and J, I don't know why, they are just cool,
I love watching the sunrise and the sunset,
I'm not like normal girls and I know it,
But that's fine because I am who I am.

Hollie Difford (11)
Wadham School, Crewkerne

An English Rose

An English rose stands alone in a field of daisies
Stormy grey eyes pierce the crystal skies
Light brown hair falls to below her shoulders
Dark skinny jeans fall wide at her ankles
A pale blue jumper shrouds her slim shoulders

A mysterious figure stands at the edge of the picture
But at the centre of her mind, whispering to her comfortingly
She doesn't know it yet, but he stands on her timeline in the near future

Her youngest sister skips through the daisies, content
Her parents stand either side of her, a family
Two cats slink around her ankles and purr
And she is content
An English rose in a field of daisies.

Phoebe Curtis (11)
Wadham School, Crewkerne

The Beautiful Game

Courtois' fearless driving
Ramos' merciless tackling
Iniesta's calm passing
Messi's unstoppable free kicks
Ronaldo's ruthless finishing
Neymar's silky skills
Modric's beautiful passing
Musiala's never-ending energy
Kroos' accurate through-balls
Van Dijk's amazing defending
Son's dangerous dribbling
Kane's accurate penalties
Haaland's record-breaking goals
Mbappé's incredible pace
Vinicius' intelligent runs
There are so many legends of the beautiful game
If they can do it, so can you.

Charlie Hughes (11)
Wadham School, Crewkerne

My World

A crochet blanket,
So soft, so warm,
Inside are things I love.
Let's have a peek inside.

Cinammon swirls line the edges with strawberries on top.
Mango and kiwi I love dearly.
Paper dragons welcome me in,
They say come in, there is much to explore.
We come to a zoo where animals roam free,
Jumping spiders and snakes galore.
We move on to horses, bees and mice.

Now we move on to sports,
Rock climbing, swimming as well.
As we soar past them, we find nature,
So peaceful, so calm.
I fall asleep so fast to dream happy dreams.

Sienna Madgin (11)
Wadham School, Crewkerne

Me

Hi, my name's Ella
And this is all about...
Me!

I give a hug to penguins,
But run away from spiders.
I like p-p-p-penguins,
I like pasta with meatballs too.
So that's what I like and dislike.

I dance all night long,
Singing and dancing too,
That is what I do.

Sometimes happy,
Sometimes sad,
Sometimes hangry,
Sometimes lonely,
That's the way I am.

Dotting dots,
Reading lots,
Hugging,
Dancing,
Singing,
Writing,
Pasta,

Penguins,
That is all,
Me!

Ella Priddle (11)
Wadham School, Crewkerne

A Friend

In the corner of the room
Sat all alone
A friend I'll have, till the tone
Who never answers her phone

Emma, who always supports me
And on her birthday went down to the sea

Emma, who is always there
And always stands out with her bright ginger hair

Emma, who makes me feel good
And sat with me on a big pile of wood

Emma, who picks me up when I'm down
And who makes me laugh, when I frown

And now we're both older
And speak even more
I need her more than ever
Emma, just like before.

Edie Pattisson
Wadham School, Crewkerne

I'm Just Me

I'm not rich and famous
I'm not smart and popular
I'm not surrounded by people
I'm just me
I'm a girl who is basic and bright
I'm kind and helpful
I'm strong and brave
I'm just me
I'm no popstar or model
I'm no famous TV star
I'm no singer or dancer
I'm just me
And if I'm not enough
Please just let me be.

Poppy Dennis (11)
Wadham School, Crewkerne

Darcie Is Amazing

D etermined
A mazing
R espectful
C aring
I ndependent
E xtraordinary

I ntelligent
S uper

A mbitious
M isunderstood
A dventurous
Z oo is my favourite hobby
I ndigo is my favourite colour
N ice
G reat.

Darcie Charlton (12)
Wadham School, Crewkerne

This Is Me

T he name is Arabella,
H ello, hi, whatever you like,
I love cats, that's me,
S unshine follows me,

I n my quest to always be happy,
S miling, singing, also South African.

M urders, mysteries in
E very book.

That's just all me!

Arabella Linten (11)
Wadham School, Crewkerne

Oliver's Sloths

O h,
L ively
I like the park
V isiting new places
E nvironment
R ace car
S leepy

S afe
L ovely
O ften
T ea
H opeful
S leepover.

Oliver Newbery (12)
Wadham School, Crewkerne

Music Is Life

M y life has changed from listening to music
U nbearable pain was healed from it
S ad thoughts and hard times were fixed with it
I t helped me build my future
C omforting me when nothing else could.

Mykie Greenhill (14)
Wadham School, Crewkerne

All About Katelin

K ittens playing with me
A little annoying
T alking to my friends
E njoy going out with my family
L ounging around in my PJs
I nterested in horse riding
N ot liking lasagne.

Katelin White (12)

Wadham School, Crewkerne

This Is Me

C ute and cuddly
A dventurous and active
T hankful and tiny
S trong and special.

Cats are kind, cats are strong,
Cats are cute, cats are cuddly.
And they always will be.

Leah Coombes (12)
Wadham School, Crewkerne

What Truly Makes Me?

Is it friends and family, maybe?
Is is my hobbies and the things I love?
Is it the movies that shape the way I think?
Or is it the fears that keep me away?
Truly, what makes me is my personality.

Isaac Galfin (13)
Wadham School, Crewkerne

Silly Sophie

S   illy like a monkey

O   utstanding like a champion

P   ositive like a panda

H   uggable like a dog

I   mpressive like a peacock

E   legant like an eagle.

Sophie Venn (12)

Wadham School, Crewkerne

Me!

I may not be the best,
I may not be the top story,
I may not be a hero,
I may not be the coolest,
I may not be the smartest,
I may not be the most popular,
But this is me.

Stanley Glover (13)
Wadham School, Crewkerne

This Is Me

T   all
H   ungry
I   ntelligent
S   porty, very sporty

I   mpressive
S   mart

M   isunderstood
E   motional.

Faith Parsons (13)
Wadham School, Crewkerne

Cats

C ats, they come in all sizes
A cat can be calm or mental
T hey can be a pain sometimes
S ome say they make your day.

Carl Bowles (15)
Wadham School, Crewkerne

Me

C ool
A gile
L oyal
E nergetic
B oy.

Caleb Russell (12)

Wadham School, Crewkerne

Sami's Poem

S tupid
A dventurous
M arvellous
I ntelligent.

Sami Malik (11)
Wadham School, Crewkerne

This Is Me

J oyful
A dventurous
C ool
K ind and cool.

Jack Smith (12)
Wadham School, Crewkerne

YOUNG WRITERS INFORMATION

We hope you have enjoyed reading this book – and that you will continue to in the coming years.

If you're the parent or family member of an enthusiastic poet or story writer, do visit our website **www.youngwriters.co.uk/subscribe** and sign up to receive news, competitions, writing challenges and tips, activities and much, much more! There's lots to keep budding writers motivated!

If you would like to order further copies of this book, or any of our other titles, then please give us a call or order via your online account.

Young Writers
Remus House
Coltsfoot Drive
Peterborough
PE2 9BF
(01733) 890066
info@youngwriters.co.uk

 YoungWritersUK   YoungWritersCW

 youngwriterscw   youngwriterscw

SCAN THE QR CODE TO WATCH THE THIS IS ME VIDEO!